How to Sell Fitness Without Selling Your Soul

A No BS Sales System for Fitness Professionals
and Gym Owners Who Hate Selling

TOM LEONARDIS JR.

Published by Leonardis Publishing Co.
New Egypt, New Jersey

Published in the United States of America

First Edition

For Kristin, Hailey, and Hudson.

You do not build an engine so people can hear it.
You build it so the people you love
never have to push the car.

Kristin, you are the reason any of this works.
Hailey and Hudson, everything I build is so you
never have to wonder what it looks like
when someone refuses to quit.

I love you three more than you will ever know.

HOW TO USE THIS BOOK

Read this book in order the first time. Every chapter builds on the one before it. The mindset chapters set the foundation. The system chapters give you the tools. The objection chapters prepare you for the moments that matter most. The close brings it all together.

Then go back and use it as a reference. Appendix A has the full qualifying call script, word for word. Appendix B has the Objection Playbook with nine objections and three responses each. The Weekly Scoreboard has the five numbers you check every Monday. The Your Move sections at the end of every chapter are your working documents.

This book was written to be used, not just read. Dog ear the pages. Write in the margins. Tear out the worksheets. Tape the scripts next to your phone. The people who get the most out of this are the ones who treat it like a manual, not a memoir.

One last thing. I cannot wait to hear from the people who read this book. If something in here changes the way you sell, the way you think, or the way you show up, I want to know about it. Send me an email and I will write you back. That is not a line. I mean it.

CONTENTS

The Night I Shushed My Daughter

It was 7 PM on a Tuesday and I was supposed to be chasing my daughter around the house.

We have this thing, Hailey and me. We have a big open floor plan and she makes me chase her in circles around the stairs. She squeals. I pretend to be slower than I am.

She thinks she is winning. It is the best part of my day.

But that Tuesday, I was on the phone. A prospect I had been chasing for weeks had finally called back. I was standing in the kitchen, pacing, doing that thing where you talk with your hands even though nobody can see you.

And Hailey came up to me. She tugged on my shirt. She wanted to play.

I shushed her.

Not aggressively. Not meanly. Just a quick finger to the lips. Shhh. Daddy's on a call.

She walked away. And I kept talking. I closed the deal. Good call. Felt productive.

But that night, after I put her to bed, I sat in the kitchen and something hit me. Not like a lightbulb. More like a slow crack in something I had been trying to hold together.

Because here is the thing nobody tells you about grinding: you can justify anything in business until it shows up in your living room. That is when it gets real. And that is when your why either holds or it does not.

A few weeks later, my son Hudson did something that finished the job.

He is 18 months old. Can barely talk. But he found Hailey's old toy phone and started walking around the house with it pressed to his ear. Pacing. Talking gibberish. Doing exactly what he had been watching me do every single day.

Everyone laughed. My wife took a video. It was cute.

It hit me like a truck.

They are not listening to what you say. They are watching how you live.

And sometimes you have to look in the mirror and ask yourself a question that does not have a comfortable answer: Who am I becoming?

Why This Book Exists

Here is the part of the book where most authors tell you about themselves. I am going to keep it short.

I have never owned a gym. What I have done, since I was 17 years old, is run them. Rescue them. Rebuild them.

Every gym I walked into I treated like it was my own. The difference is I had to prove my worth every single time with nothing but results.

I have a Master's degree in Exercise Science with a concentration in biomechanics. None of that mattered until I figured out the sales and leadership side.

The degree tells you how the body works. It does not tell you how to sit across from a frightened human being and help them believe in themselves.

My first job in this industry was at New York Sports Club in Colonia, New Jersey. I lied about my age to get hired.

I loved my first boss. Then they had three different bosses in six months. New trainers every week.

Staff walking out the door before they learned anybody's name. I was 17 years old watching a business bleed out in front of me.

I was young enough to see it clearly because I had not yet learned how to make excuses for it.

That revolving door taught me the most important thing I know about building anything worth building.

"Get help while building your vision. Not while you are trying to

save it."

Since then I have been inside of every kind of room this industry has: big box, boutique, small group, one on one, corporate, mom and pop.

I have seen owners lose everything because they would not have a real conversation about the sales floor.

I have seen owners triple their revenue in six months because they finally did.

This book is the conversation I wish somebody had sat me down and forced me through when I was 25.

The methodology in it is not theory. I have trained it, stress tested it, and watched people use it to save their businesses.

Who This Book Is For

I wrote this for anyone in sales. But specifically for people in the business of changing lives.

The gym owner wearing every hat. The trainer who loves helping people but freezes at the money conversation. The appointment setter whose calls keep ending with a ghost.

And anyone in fitness adjacent businesses who sells transformation. The conversations are the same. The objections are the same.

The psychology behind every yes and every no is the same.

Be needed. Not needy.

Let us go.

- Tom Leonardis Jr.

Before you can sell anyone else, you have to sell yourself.

PART ONE

THE MINDSET

"You can have everything in life you want, if you will just help enough other people get what they want."

— Zig Ziglar

CHAPTER ONE

You Are the Product

Why the "best you" always sells

"Your most important sale is the one you make to yourself every single day."

— Dan Kennedy

there is a book I really like called Eat What You Kill by Sam Taggart. Sam is the founder of D2D Experts and built a seven figure business knocking on doors for a living.

Think about that for a second. This man would walk up to a stranger's house, knock on the door, and try to convince someone to buy something they never asked for.

We do not have to do that. Our people are coming to us. They already have a problem.

They already want help.

they are scrolling at 11 PM on their couch, they see our ad, and they raise their hand. They fill out a form. They text us. They show up.

And still, most of us struggle to close them. Not because we are bad salespeople. Because we are showing up wrong.

we are tired, we are distracted, and we are dragging every problem we have into that conversation. The person on the other end notices.

So before I teach you a single script, framework, or closing technique, I need you to understand one thing. You are the product.

And the best version of you always sells.

The Six Rules of the Sales Carnivore

I adapted these from Sam's book and from 20 years of doing this. These are not suggestions. They are the rules.

Break them and you lose sales. Follow them and the work gets easier.

Rule 1. You create leads. You do not wait.

Carnivores do not sit by the phone hoping someone calls. They prospect. They network. They follow up.

They drive traffic to themselves. Every single day there is an action. Check a new Facebook group. Send messages. Make something happen.

You do not sit still. Ever.

Rule 2. You sell the problem, not the program.

People are not buying your training packages. They are buying solutions to pain.

Weight gain. Fear. Embarrassment. Weakness. The feeling of being invisible to their own family.

That is what they want gone. Sell that and the program sells itself.

Rule 3. You treat objections as buying signals.

When someone says I need to think about it or it is the money, that is not a no. That is them still in the conversation.

Objections mean they want you to convince them. Carnivores see objections as part of the close, not the end of it.

Rule 4. You train your pitch like an athlete.

You role play. You do script work. You practice your tonality. You record your calls and you listen back.

If Kobe Bryant practiced fadeaway jumpers at 5 AM you can practice your opening line.

Rule 5. You use silence strategically.

Most salespeople cannot sit there after they ask a question. Three seconds of silence feels like a minute and they start filling the air.

Silence is pressure. Silence is a question still hanging there. Ask your question and let it sit.

The next person to talk loses. Let it be them.

Rule 6. You believe closing is coaching.

You are not manipulating anyone. You are guiding them to make the best decision for their own life.

The best closers operate from service, not from need. That is the whole game.

Where This Phrase Comes From

Early in my sales career I came across as needy. I was young, I needed the money, and it showed on every call.

I had a boss I butted heads with constantly. We argued about everything. But he eventually helped me find the value I had in myself.

He made me understand something that changed everything. The prospect needs you. You do not need them.

Once that clicked, the chasing stopped. The pressure stopped. And closing started happening, because the prospect could feel it too.

Let me tell you a story that made the concept stick for me forever.

I went to dinner with someone once who asked me questions the entire night. I talked the whole time.

When I finally looked down at my plate, my food was untouched. Theirs was gone.

I walked out of that restaurant thinking that was the best conversation I had ever had in my life. And I had barely heard a thing about them.

That is what a great closer does. They ask questions and disappear into them.

They make the whole conversation about the person across the table. By the time the check comes the other person has already sold themselves.

"A genius conversationalist is somebody who can talk to

somebody about them and only about them."

You are going to see me reference this concept in the Closing. I am not going to beat you over the head with the phrase itself in between.

Just know this. Every chapter from here to the end is built on top of it.

The $60 Reframe

Here is a mindset shift that changed everything for me.

Say you have 100 leads. For every 100 leads, you sell one client. That client's lifetime value is $6,000.

Do the math. $6,000 divided by 100 leads equals $60 per lead.

Every single person who says no to you just generated $60 toward that eventual $6,000 close. Every no is one step closer to a yes.

When you think about it this way, rejection stops being personal and starts being math. Math does not care about your feelings.

What People Really Buy

People do not buy your programs. They do not buy trainers. They do not buy testimonials.

People buy states. They buy the gap between who they are today and who they want to be six months from now.

Here are the states people actually buy.

"I am overweight and I hate how I look. I want to feel lean and confident."

"I am weak and injury prone. I want to feel strong and resilient."

"I am isolated and unmotivated. I want to feel connected and part of something."

"I am insecure and self conscious. I want to feel proud of who I am."

"I am exhausted all the time. I want to wake up feeling alive."

Emotions drive decisions more than logic. If you get someone emotional, they will buy.

Male, female, it does not matter. Emotion is the fuel. Logic is the justification they give their spouse after the fact.

The Woman Who Never Lost a Pound

We had a woman at one of the gyms I ran who had been coming for six years. I never saw her lose any weight in that entire time.

Not a pound. But she has been there every single day for six years. Why?

Because she has everything else. We bust her chops every day. She laughs harder than anyone in the room.

She is connected. She is part of something. The weight loss was never the real thing she was buying.

Certainty and significance are the king and queen of sales. If someone is certain it will work and they feel significant being there, they will stay forever.

Build Internal Pressure, Not External

There is a difference between internal pressure and external pressure, and most salespeople get it backwards.

Internal pressure is when the prospect hears themselves say I cannot keep living like this. External pressure is when you say the sale ends Friday.

Your job is to build internal pressure by asking questions that make the person realize, on their own, that they cannot stay where they are.

"If you do not do anything for the next six months, how are you going to feel?"

That is not a sales tactic. That is a coaching question.

When they hear themselves say probably heavier and more frustrated, you did not put pressure on them. You held up a mirror.

Say It Back To Them

There is one more rule inside this one. If they say it, it is the truth. If you say it, it is a pitch.

Remember that every time you are tempted to tell them why they should buy. Instead, get them to tell you.

Known In Every Gym Within Driving Distance

The only guarantee a Facebook ad gives you is that at 9 PM on a Tuesday, somebody sitting on their couch is going to see your name.

The way you make that ad 10 times more powerful is simple. Become known in every gym within driving distance.

When they see your ad they should already have seen you in their chiropractor's office. At their kid's baseball game. At the local coffee shop.

You are part of their world. That is the ad that actually works.

Get out of the four walls. Every time you think about it, you are going to cringe and want to run back inside. Do it anyway.

The Long Game

Here is something nobody wants to hear. Only 15 percent of your leads will buy in the first 100 days. The other 85 percent will buy in the next three years.

We had a guy sign up who had been on our email list since 2017. Eight years. It took him eight years to pull the trigger.

The long game pays off. Some clients take years to say yes. Keep following up. Keep sending value. Keep showing up.

Because the moment you stop showing up is the moment they forget you exist.

YOUR MOVE

Grab a pen. This is where the work happens.

1. On a scale of 1 to 10, how strong are your sales skills right now? Write the number.

2. Look at the Six Rules. Which one do you need most right now? Circle it.

3. Think about the last time a bad call ruined your next call. What happened?

4. Do the $60 math for your own business. Write the number on a sticky note. Put it next to your phone.

5. What are you doing to be known in every gym within driving distance? List three local spots you could walk into this week.

____

____

____

6. Write down the current state and the desired state of your ideal client.

____

____

____

7. Are you showing up needed or needy? Think about your last three sales conversations. Be brutally honest.

____

____

____

CHAPTER TWO

Installing A Sales Mindset

The 5 step mental framework that changes everything

"If I could tattoo something on everybody's forehead so they would see it every time they looked in the mirror, it would be this: they need you more than you need them."

— Tom Leonardis Jr.

Every framework in this book starts in your head before it comes out of your mouth. Installing A Sales Mindset is where it all begins.

I am not someone who follows a script well. Never have been. But when I can see something in my mind and make it my own, I become a completely different person on the phone.

So I asked myself: what do I actually do before every call, every consult, every conversation that matters? What is happening inside my head when I am at my best?

Five things. Five mental steps that I go through before I pick up the phone, before I sit down across from someone, before I open my mouth.

Visualize. Create. Clear the Mechanism. Shift. Drive.

That is the framework. That is the Installing A Sales Mindset. And once you start running it, your conversations will never sound the same again.

Step 1: Visualize

Most people think visualization in sales means picturing the credit card swipe. Seeing the signed contract. Imagining the commission hitting your account.

That is not what this is.

Visualizing is about seeing the person. The actual human being who is about to be on the other end of that phone or sitting across from you. You visualize their answers as if you have known them for years.

You are listening so deeply in your mind that somewhere inside you, you already know the answer they are searching for before they even say it.

You have to see their heaven island, their success, more clearly than they see their current hell island. That is the level you need to operate at. They are stuck in their pain.

They cannot see past it. But you can. And when you walk into that conversation already seeing the outcome for them, everything changes. Your tone changes. Your questions change. Your energy changes.

Before your next call, close your eyes for 60 seconds. Picture the person on the other end. Not as a lead.

Not as a number on your scoreboard. As a person who is struggling with something real and hoping you are the one who can help. See them six months from now, after they have done the work.

See the smile. See the confidence. That is what you are selling them.

If you can see it for them before they can see it for themselves, they will trust you. Because you are not guessing. You are certain.

Step 2: Create

Now you are the architect.

This is the stage where you build the emotional bridge. You are not winging it. You are not hoping the conversation goes well.

You are creating the entire arc in your mind before it happens. From the initial text message, to the qualifying call, to the consult, to the sale, to the 12 month resign.

You use the right questions at the right times, in the right tones. Up, down, soft, direct. You bring them closer to their own realization that they actually need you.

Not that you need them. You are creating a path where every question leads to the next, and the next, and the next, until they arrive at the decision on their own. Think about what happens when you do not create.

You show up flat. You say, "Hey, come on in for a consultation, we will set you up." The last thing someone wants to hear is that they need to come get told what is wrong with them. That is what it sounds like when you have not created the conversation in advance.

But when you have built the bridge? When you know where the conversation is going and you guide them there with intention? They feel it. They lean in. They start telling you things they have never told anyone.

And that is when you know you have done your job. That is the craft.

Step 3: Clear the Mechanism

This is the hardest one. And I am still practicing it.

There is a movie called For Love of the Game with Kevin Costner. He plays a pitcher, and right before he throws, he says to himself, "Clear the mechanism." And in that moment, the entire stadium goes silent. The crowd disappears. The noise is gone.

All that is left is the target.

That is what you have to do before every call.

Think about all the noise you carry into a conversation. Your kid is sick. Your mom is in the hospital.

Someone you thought was going to close just quit. You just lost five clients. Rent is due. You had a fight with your spouse.

Your last three calls went nowhere.

Now imagine picking up the phone with all of that sitting on your shoulders. What do you think that person hears? They hear desperation. They hear distraction. They hear someone who needs them more than they need you.

You have to empty out that entire database of noise.

All of it. Because none of it matters if you really want to help the person on the other end of that line.

I like to think of it like a scary movie. You know how scary movies work, right? The music is doing 90% of the work.

The creepy sounds, the sudden loud notes, the whispering. But if you cover your ears and remove the noise? It is not even scary anymore.

It is just someone walking through a dark hallway.

That is what picking up the phone is. It is just a conversation. Remove the noise and it is just you helping another person. That is it.

So before your call block, before you pick up the phone, before you sit down for a consult: write down everything that is in your head. Everything. The bills.

The stress. The bad call from this morning. Write it all down. Then crumple it up and throw it in the garbage.

Physically do it. Get it out of your body.

Be present. Your bills get paid when you focus on what you can control. If you focus on what you cannot control, you are always going to be running in circles trying to catch up.

Step 4: Shift

Now you take whatever noise is left and you turn it into a desired outcome. This is the mindset shift that separates people who burn out from people who build. Instead of going into a call thinking "I need to get this client," you shift to "I get to help this person." Every phone call is a potential life changing moment for the person on the other end of the line.

Not for you. For them. They are the one who has been laying in bed at night thinking about how their clothes do not fit. They are the one whose doctor just told them their blood pressure is too high. They are the one who cannot keep up with their kids.

Your job is to bridge the gap to their heaven island. Not to widen it through self sabotage, pushiness, or letting your own needs overshadow their desires.

They do not know how to get there. That is why they are on the phone with you. That is why they are up at 10 o'clock at night searching for answers.

When you shift from getting to helping, the entire energy of the conversation changes. You slow down. You listen better. You ask deeper questions. And the person on the other end can feel it.

They feel safe. They feel heard. And people who feel heard are people who buy.

Step 5: Drive

The path you create is the roadmap. But like any map, there are going to be unforeseen bumps in the road. If you are from Jersey, you know about potholes the size of your car. They just happen.

There are no shortcuts or handouts. If a shortcut was the way, it would just be the way. You have to go down the path.

You have to give them the vision, the direction they need to go to be successful.

Here is what happens in real life: you are going to get distracted. You are going to fall off. Someone's going to hang up on you.

A consult that was a sure thing is going to walk out. A client you have had for two years is going to cancel.

That is not the question. The question is: how fast can you get back on the road?

The speed in which you start the car back up is determined by how fast you can clear the mechanism. If you just got hung up on, how fast can you get back into the vision of "I am going this way"? If you just lost a client, how quickly can you reset and show up fully for the next person?

That is what makes the difference. When you are locked in, the client feels your commitment. It drives frequency and accountability.

But if you are not locked in? They can hear it. They know you are needy.

And needy does not close.

The Five Steps in Practice

Here is what Installing A Sales Mindset looks like in real time. You are about to start your call block. Maybe it is 8 AM.

You have got 10 calls to make.

Step 1: Close your eyes. Visualize the first person on your list. See them as a real human with a real problem. See their outcome. See their success.

Step 2: Create the arc of the conversation in your head. What are you going to ask? How are you going to guide them?

Where does the conversation need to go?

Step 3: Clear the mechanism. Write down every piece of noise in your head. Crumple it up. Throw it away. The stadium is silent now.

Step 4: Shift your intention. You are not here to close. You are here to help.

Say it out loud if you have to: "This call is for them, not for me."

Step 5: Drive. Make the call. Stay locked in. And when it is over, whether it went great or terrible, clear the mechanism again and do it for the next one.

Do this before every call block. Every consult. Every conversation that matters. It takes five minutes.

And it will change the way people respond to you.

YOUR MOVE

Grab a pen. This is where the work happens.

1. Before your next call, practice the full 5 step Installing A Sales Mindset. Write down how it felt compared to how you normally show up.

---

2. CLEAR THE MECHANISM: Write every piece of noise in your head right now. Everything. Bills, stress, bad calls, personal stuff. Get it all out. Now rip this page out and throw it away. (Yes, literally.)

---

3. SHIFT: Rewrite your intention for your next call block. Replace "I need to close" with something that starts with "I get to help."

CHAPTER THREE

The Four Energy Drivers

How to show up like a pro every single day

"Success is not for the weary. It is for those who show up every day ready to fight."

— Grant Cardone

I am going to tell you something that might piss you off. Your worst sales weeks are not lead problems. They are energy problems.

I hear the same things from gym owners and trainers every single week. My leads are garbage. Nobody's answering. I cannot get anyone to commit.

Here is the truth. The leads did not change. What changed is you.

What you can control is how you show up when the phone rings. When your energy is in the gutter, everything tanks.

The leads do not suck. You just suck right now. And that is okay.

Because it is fixable.

The Month I Was Living With My In Laws

I want to tell you about May.

Going through a remodel with your wife is tough. Going through a remodel with two kids is tougher.

Going through a remodel of your own house while living with your in laws for a month? That was May for me.

I was making sales calls from my son's bedroom. No toilets in my actual house.

Construction workers were breaking tile and banging for ten hours straight outside the window I was trying to close deals through.

If you remember from earlier in this book, leaving your stuff at the door is non negotiable.

It is one of the rules. I believe that. I teach it.

But here is what I can tell you from experience. Sometimes the stuff bleeds in anyway.

I was distracted on calls. I was short with people. My energy was wrong and the people on the other end could feel it.

So what got me out of it? A Tom Hanks interview.

He was asked how he handles the highs and lows of 40 plus years in the public eye. He said something I believe comes from the Bible, though he never cited it.

I wrote it down on a piece of paper and put it on the desk where I was making calls.

"This too shall pass."

Think about what that actually means for you in sales. When you are in the worst streak of your life, when nothing is working, this too shall pass.

But here is the other side of it that most people miss.

When you are on a hot streak, when everything feels easy, when you are signing people up every week... this too shall pass.

It works in both directions. It keeps you humble when you are winning and grounded when you are losing.

The construction eventually stopped. We moved back in. The new offer got refined. May ended.

And I came out of it with a better business than I went in with. That is the scoreboard that actually matters.

The Four Energy Drivers

There are four energy drivers that determine how you show up. Not just on sales calls. In everything.

When all four are above a 7 out of 10, you are unstoppable. When any of them drops below a 7, you are going to feel it. So will every person you talk to.

Driver 1: Physiology

Are you moving daily? Are you sleeping well? Are you eating real food?

Are you staying hydrated? The basics.

When I am not doing those things, I am not paying attention the way I need to.

Build your morning ritual. Build your evening ritual. Get your head right before you touch the phone.

Driver 2: Clarity

Do you know exactly where the business is going? In May, nothing had changed except me.

I had lost clarity. I was doing a lot of things but I was not clear on why any of them mattered.

When you have clarity, you know what to do when you wake up. When you do not, you are just spinning.

Driver 3: Necessity

Why does this matter to you? Is there a deeper reason behind the grind?

Necessity is the fire. It is what gets you out of bed when you do not feel like it.

It is what makes you pick up the phone for the 47th time even though the last 46 went to voicemail.

If your necessity score is low, your why is probably too surface level. Chapter 4 will help you fix that.

Driver 4: Inspiration

What are you consuming daily? I have an hour and fifteen minute drive to the office and I use every minute of it.

Audiobooks. Podcasts. Something that lights me up before I step into the building.

If you are spending your morning scrolling Instagram or watching the news, you are poisoning your mindset before you say good morning to a lead.

What you put in is what comes out on the call.

Identify the Dip

When things go sideways, do not panic. Do not blame the leads. Start here.

Which energy driver is below a 7? Score yourself on all four. Find the one that is lowest.

That is your dip. That is what is dragging everything else down.

Then ask yourself. What was I doing three weeks ago when things were better? Go do that.

Leave Work at Work

When the day is done, leave it. Do not bring the bad calls home. Do not bring the stress of the pipeline into your living room.

do not be on your phone checking texts while your kid is trying to show you a drawing.

I shushed my daughter because I could not separate work from home. My family does not care about my close rate. They care about whether Dad is present.

YOUR MOVE

Grab a pen. This is where the work happens.

1. Rate your four drivers right now. Physiology, clarity, necessity, inspiration. Each one out of 10.

____

____

____

2. Which driver is your lowest? Be honest.

____

____

____

3. What is one thing you can do this week to move it up two points?

____

____

____

4. Write this too shall pass on a card and put it on your desk. Look at it tomorrow morning.

____

____

____

CHAPTER FOUR

Finding Your Why

And leaving your wallet at the door

"If you do not know why you do what you do, how will you know when you have done it?"

— Sabri Suby

I used to say my family was my why. It sounded right. It felt right. You provide, you protect, you win.

But if I am honest, that was not the real why. The real driver was my fear of failing. And there is a difference.

I love money. I love building. I love helping people. That is why I got into this industry 20 years ago. None of that is wrong.

But none of that is a why.

Those are outcomes. A why has to anchor you. It has to define how you win. Not how much you make.

Not how many clients you close. How you win as a person. Think about why your clients stay with you. They are winning. If you do not know what you are winning, why would they stay?

If you do not know what you are building toward, you will just keep building and eventually you will not like what you built.

The Problem with a Clean Why

Most people's whys are too clean. They are rehearsed. They sound good on a stage or in a bio but they do not do anything when you are sitting alone in your car at 7 AM trying to convince yourself to make 50 phone calls.

"I want to help people." That is not a why. That is a job description. "I want to provide for my family." That is closer. But provide what? A paycheck? A lifestyle? Safety? Dig deeper.

"I want to make more money." That is a goal. Not a why. Money is an outcome. It is fuel. It is not the engine.

A real why is messy. It is uncomfortable. It makes you feel something when you say it out loud. If your why does not make your stomach turn a little bit, it is not deep enough.

You have not gotten there yet.

How I Found Mine

I will tell you about my brother in law in the next chapter. That story belongs there, next to everything I have to say about money and the cost of getting that relationship wrong.

My why today is my mom. She is 77 years old. She cannot pick up my kids and stand up at the same time.

She cannot watch them by herself. And that bothers me. Deeply.

I see clients every day who are my mom's age and they can outlift her, outwalk her, outlast her.

They have what she does not and it is not money or luck. It is the body they trained for 30 years. She did not.

My father lost the house I grew up in. The house his great grandfather built. Gone. Financial struggles. Money fights.

I made a promise to myself that my kids would never live in a house where the adults argued about whether we could afford groceries.

Notice something? None of my whys are about helping other people in some vague generic way.

They are about pain. Loss. Fear. Things I never want to experience again and things I never want my family to experience.

That is what a real why sounds like.

Noah's Eviction Notice

One of my sales training program students, Noah, told me his why during a live session. And it is one of the best examples I have ever heard.

Before he and his wife had kids, they were living in Florida and struggling. One day they came home to an eviction notice on the door. He could not make rent.

He made it work somehow. But when their first child was born, he made a vow: that would never happen again.

I told him to print out a picture of that eviction notice. Put it on his sun visor. Stick it on his laptop.

Put it on his bathroom mirror. Put it everywhere he is going to see it. Because when the calls are not going his way and the leads feel cold and he is thinking about giving up for the day, that piece of paper is going to remind him exactly why he cannot.

The next day, he booked three consults. All we did was shift his mindset. We did not change a single thing about his script, his leads, or his process.

We just reminded him why he was doing it.

Why a Clean Why Does not Work on

Calls

Here is the practical side of this. When your why is not defined, none of the tactics in this book will stick. Because clarity drives discipline.

Discipline builds systems. And systems create freedom.

If you go into a call without a why, you are just making calls. You are going through the motions. You are asking questions because you are supposed to, not because you actually care about the answers.

And the person on the other end can feel that.

But when your why is locked in? When you know exactly what you are building toward and what is at stake if you do not? You show up differently.

Your questions are sharper. Your patience is longer. Your conviction is unshakeable.

And people trust conviction. They buy from people who believe in something bigger than the sale.

If anything from this entire book sticks with you, let it be this chapter. Hold on to your why. Write it down. Post it somewhere you will see it every single day.

Because when you feel like you just got the shit kicked out of you and no one even touched you, look at that list and remind yourself: it was not that bad.

Get back up. There is someone on the other end of that next call who needs you.

The Five Questions

I am going to ask you five questions. They are not comfortable. They are not meant to be.

Take your time. Be honest. Do not write the polished version.

Write the raw one.

1. What pulled you into this industry? Not the career path. Not the opportunity. What was the moment, the person, or the event that made you say, "This is what I am supposed to do"?

2. What pain are you protecting other people from? Is there a loss, a failure, or an experience that you never want someone else to go through? That is usually where the deepest whys live.

3. What scares you more than rejection? Getting hung up on is annoying. What is actually terrifying?

Losing your house? Your kids seeing you fail? Your parents worrying about you? Go there.

4. What legacy are you building? Not what do you want to be remembered for. What do you want your kids, your family, or the people who matter most to see when they watch how you live?

5. If you stopped today, who would it hurt the most? Not you. Someone else. Who depends on you showing up? Who benefits from you not quitting?

That is your why.

What Money Actually Taught Me

Growing up the way I did taught me three things that I carry into every sales conversation I have.

The first is that money cannot buy you happiness. I know that sounds like a bumper sticker but I watched it play out in real time. Objects are just objects.

Wearing something expensive or driving an expensive car, if you cannot actually afford it, means nothing. Less than nothing, because it costs you sleep and security and eventually the things that actually matter.

The second is that your relationship with money will hold you back in sales if you do not deal with it. If someone says "I do not know if I have that right now" and you immediately back down because you project your own financial fears onto them, you will never close at the level you are capable of. The person in front of you might have spent $250 at Starbucks this week.

You do not know. It is not your job to decide whether they can afford it. It is your job to help them decide whether they want it badly enough.

The third is that what you do with money defines you more than how much of it you make.

Why This Matters on Every Sales Call

When you walk into a consultation or pick up the phone, your financial situation has to stay in the car. It does not come inside with you. It does not sit at the table.

It does not influence the words coming out of your mouth. Because the second your own money fears start talking, you lose.

Here is how it shows up: someone tells you what they want, you know you can help them, you know your program is worth every dollar, and then the moment comes where you have to say the price. And you flinch. You soften. You start discounting before they even ask. You throw in a "but we can work something out" before they have said a single word.

That is not them having a problem with your price. That is you having a problem with your price.

I see it all the time. Gym owners and trainers who undercharge because they are projecting their own financial fears onto their clients. They think, I would not pay that much, so they assume nobody else will either.

But you are not the client. Your bank account is not their bank account. Your story is not their story.

> *"People spend $5 a day at Starbucks without thinking about it.*
> *That is $150 a month on coffee. But you are sweating over*
> *asking someone to invest $500 a month to change their life?"*

The price is not the problem. The value you have built is the problem. If they see the value, they will find the money.

People always find money for the things they actually want.

Know What Your Time Is Worth

I know what my time is worth. I am not training anyone one on one for less than $200 an hour. I do not care if I never train another person again.

That is my number. And a lot of people pay it.

You need to know yours. Not what you think the market will tolerate. Not what the gym down the street charges.

What your time, your expertise, and your energy are actually worth.

Think about it this way: how much is your time away from your kids worth? How much is missing bedtime worth? How much is driving 45 minutes to train one person for $40 actually worth when you do the real math?

When you answer that honestly, you start to realize that most people are dramatically undercharging. And the reason is not the market. It is their own money story.

When you walk into a room knowing your number, owning it, and believing it in your gut, the person across from you can feel that. They trust it. They respect it. Because confidence in your price is confidence in your ability to deliver results. And that is what they are actually buying.

Leave Your Wallet at the Door

Every time I walk into a consultation, my wallet stays in the car. Figuratively. I do not think about my mortgage. I do not think about my car payment.

I do not think about what I would or would not pay for something. None of that matters.

What matters is the person in front of me, what they need, and what it is going to take to get them there. When I write the prescription, I write it based on what they need. Not what I think they can afford.

The moment I start making financial assumptions for someone else, I have lost them. I am no longer a coach. I am a salesperson who is afraid of his own prices.

"When I walk into that room, I do not even own a bank account. It is go time."

That is the mindset. You are there to help someone change their life. The price is part of the process.

It is the investment required to get from Hell Island to Heaven Island. Own it like a doctor writing a prescription. You do not see your doctor apologize for the cost of the medication.

They tell you what you need and you figure out the rest.

Fix your relationship with money and your close rate will fix itself.

YOUR MOVE

Grab a pen. This is where the work happens.

1. What pulled you into this industry?

2. What pain are you protecting other people from?

3. What scares you more than rejection?

4. What legacy are you building?

5. If you stopped today, who would it hurt the most?

____

____

____

6. Now write your raw, unpolished why. No editing. No making it sound good. Just the truth.

____

____

____

7. Where are you going to put it so you see it every single day? Write the location.

____

____

____

8. On a scale of 1 to 10, how healthy is your relationship with money right now? Be honest. Why did you give yourself that score?

____

____

____

9. What money story from your upbringing are you still carrying into your sales conversations?

____

____

____

10. What is your minimum revenue per hour? Write the number and the reason behind it.

____

____

____

11. Think about the last time you flinched on price. What happened? What did you say that you wish you had not?

____

____

____

12. Write your price statement. Practice it 10 times out loud. "Our programs range from $____ to $____ per month."

____

____

____

PART TWO

THE SYSTEM

"Every sale has five basic obstacles: no need, no money, no hurry, no desire, no trust."

— Zig Ziglar

CHAPTER FIVE

The 10 Commandments of Follow Up

Your paycheck is your pipeline

"The fortune is in the follow up."

— Dan Kennedy

The truth about sales is that most people do not lose deals because they are bad at selling. Sales are lost in silence. Not in the close.

Avoidance, fear, and inconsistency are what kill your pipeline.

I hear the same things from gym owners and trainers every single week:

"I do not want to annoy them."

"If they wanted it, they would call."

"I will follow up later."

"I do not want to seem desperate."

That is fear masking logic. And it is costing you thousands.

"The pipeline does not die from no. It dies from nothing."

If you have a fear of follow up, print that line out and tape it above your computer. Write it on your monitor with a marker if you have to.

Because the person who opted in at 10 PM last night while scrolling on their phone asked you for help.

They started this conversation. Following up is not annoying. It is finishing what they started.

Follow up is a service, not an intrusion. Reframe it in your mind as helping someone follow through on what they already asked for.

The 10 Commandments

These are non negotiable. Break them and your pipeline dies. Follow them and it thrives.

Review them weekly. Teach them to your team.

1. Your calendar is your boss. Not your feelings.

Not your mood. Not your energy level. If it says call at 8 AM, you call at 8 AM. Block your call times.

Protect them. The only exception: if a hot lead walks through your door, take the consult. Everything else can wait.

2. Broken workflows quietly cost you thousands.

Audit your CRM. Check your automated texts and emails. What worked six months ago might be stale today. If everyone thinks you are a robot, nobody's going to respond. Keep it human. Keep it fresh.

3. Never call at the same time two days in a row.

Prospects build habits fast. If you always call at 10 AM, they will memorize your number and dodge you. Vary your times. It increases your reach rate.

4. Always follow every call with a text.

If they do not answer, text immediately. Three messages, sent fast. First: "Hey [first name], this is [you] from [business].

That was me that just called." Second: Send. Third: "Would you prefer texting so I can learn more about you and what you are looking to accomplish?" Send. Bang, bang, bang.

5. Keep texts short. Texts are not your pitch deck.

Under 200 characters per send. You are starting a conversation, not writing a novel. I have seen some of your texts and they scared me.

I thought they were from an ex. Keep it tight.

6. Keep your pipeline organized.

No floating leads. Ever. Every contact needs a next step, a scheduled follow up, or a proper status in your CRM. If someone opts in, move them. Call made one. Call made two. Call made three. Whatever stages you use, use them.

You are paying for the software. Utilize it.

7. Build the seven beliefs on every call.

They have a problem. They cannot fix it alone. Doing nothing costs more.

A better future is possible. They can afford it. They have support. You are the right solution.

Use questions to lead them to these beliefs. Not pitches. When they say it, they believe it.

8. Present price as a range.

"Our programs range from $299 to $599 per month." Never say "up to." Never give a per session rate unless they ask for it. Per session math makes people multiply in their head and scare themselves. Monthly ranges feel manageable.

9. Mention your next follow up.

Do not leave it vague. Tell them: "If I do not hear from you, I will follow up again on Thursday." Set the expectation. Then follow through. If you say Thursday and you do not follow up on Thursday, you just proved you cannot be trusted.

10. Book the next step before you hang up.

On the first call, book the consult. At the consult, book the first session. Even if you do not close them, book something.

"Listen, just come try it out. I will buy your first session." Do not hang up until there is a next step on the calendar.

Separate Emotion from Execution

This is one of the hardest things to do in sales. You make five calls. Nobody answers. Two people ghost you.

One person was rude. And now you are carrying all of that into call number six.

The person on call number six did nothing to you. All they did was raise their hand and say, "Help me." They do not know about your bad morning. They do not know your last three calls went nowhere.

They deserve the best version of you, not the leftovers.

Focus on the inputs, not the outcomes. How many calls did you make? How many texts did you send?

How organized is your pipeline? Control those things. Let go of everything else. If you need to, brain dump after every 10 calls.

Write the negative thoughts out. Rip the paper.

Throw it away. Start fresh. Call the next 10.

The best salespeople in the world are not the ones who never get rejected. They are the ones who reset the fastest.

The Call Block Strategy

Here is how I structure a call block: Call 10 leads. Then take a short rest. Stand up. Stretch. Drink water. Breathe. Reset your energy. Then call 10 more.

Every call gets a clean slate. Do not let rejection carry over. Keep your tone fresh.

Avoid robotic delivery. Avoid emotional residue from a bad call.

If the first call of the day goes well, great. Do not ride that high and get sloppy. If the first call is a disaster, do not let it tank the other nine.

Each call is independent. Each person deserves your full attention.

Speed to Lead

When a lead comes in, you have less than an hour to respond. That is the reality in our industry. If someone opts in at 10 PM, you do not need to call them at 10 PM.

But you better be texting them first thing in the morning.

And if someone responds to you during business hours? You have minutes, not hours. Unless you are mid session, get back to them.

Or set the expectation: "Hey, we are in coaching sessions right now. We will be free after 3. What time after 3 works for a call?" Speed matters because the longer you wait, the colder they get.

The person who was motivated at 10 PM is half as motivated by noon the next day. And by Thursday? They have forgotten they even filled out the form.

The Fear Audit

Before we move on, I want you to be honest with yourself. Which of these fears do you carry into your follow up?

"I do not want to annoy them."

"If they wanted it, they would call."

"I will follow up later."

"I do not want to seem desperate."

Write your biggest fear down on a piece of paper. Every day before your call block, write it again. Then crumple it up and throw it in the garbage.

Do it for seven days straight. You are literally training your brain to let it go.

Because if you do not call these people, your pipeline will die. Your business will die. And everything goes along with it.

That lead did not opt in so you could be afraid. They opted in because they need you.

YOUR MOVE

Grab a pen. This is where the work happens.

1. On a scale of 1 to 10, how organized is your pipeline right now? Be honest. Score: /10 How many leads have NO next step scheduled right now? Write the number.

---

2. Grade yourself on each of the 10 Commandments (1 to 10). Circle any below a 7. 1. Calendar is my boss: 2. Workflows are current: 3. Vary call times: 4. Text after every call: 5. Texts under 200 chars: 6. Pipeline organized: 7. Build 7 beliefs: 8. Price as a range: 9. Mention next follow up: 10. Book next step

---

---

3. Write your biggest follow up FEAR from the list. Commit to writing it down and throwing it away every day for 7 days.

---

4. Write your 3 text follow up sequence (for after a missed call).

____

____

____

5. What percentage of the 10 Commandments are you actually practicing right now? Current: ____% Target by end of month: ____%

____

____

____

CHAPTER SIX

The Qualifying Call

7 minutes that determine everything

"The question is never whether you can close. It is whether you prepared to."

— Grant Cardone

This is the call that changes everything. Not the consult. Not the close. This call.

The qualifying call is where you either build enough trust to get them in the room or lose them before they ever walk through the door. Seven minutes. That is all you get. Most people waste four of them.

Here is what the seven minutes look like when done right.

The Tactical Opener

You have about thirty seconds to establish that you are a professional and that this call is worth their time. Do not waste it with small talk.

"Hey, is this [Name]? Great. This is [Your Name] from [Business]. I am giving you a call because you requested some help with a specific fitness goal you are trying to accomplish.

Does that sound right?" Two things just happened. You positioned yourself as the authority coming to them, not the desperate salesperson hoping they say yes. And you got a yes before you even started. That yes matters.

The 7 Beliefs Framework

Every qualifying call should build seven beliefs in the prospect's mind. You do not need to hit all seven in order. But by the end of the call, all seven need to be there. **Belief 1: Pain.** They must feel the weight of their current situation.

Not because you are piling on, but because they need to say it out loud to someone who is actually listening. **Belief 2: Doubt.** They must acknowledge that doing this alone is not working. Ask about what they have tried before and why it did not stick. Let them name the failure without you naming it for them. **Belief 3: Cost.** They must feel the cost of doing nothing.

Not in dollars. In life. What is another six months of this actually costing them? **Belief 4: Desire.** They must believe that solving this creates a better future. Summarize their pain, doubt, and cost in their own words. Then ask what success looks like six months from now. **Belief 5: Money.** They must believe they can make it work financially.

Not that it is cheap. That the investment makes sense relative to the cost of staying where they are. **Belief 6: Support.** They must believe the people around them will not sabotage the decision. Surface the spouse or partner question here before it surfaces at the close. **Belief 7: Trust.** They must believe you are the right person to help them.

When they say yes to belief seven, they have mentally already hired you.

Booking the Consult

When it is time to book, do not ask when they want to come in. Give them a choice between two times.

"Do you prefer mornings or evenings? I have 8 AM Monday or 6 PM Wednesday open. Which works better for you?" Two options.

Not an open calendar. Not "when works for you." Two times. People make decisions faster with limited options.

And it signals that your time is structured and your schedule is real.

When They Say They Need to Think About It

This is going to happen. A lot. Here is what I say.

"I understand. Do you need to think about it for two to three days or two to three weeks?" They almost always say two to three days. And now they have set their own follow up window. You did not chase.

They did not disappear. And the next call has a built in reason to happen.

The Science of Call Timing

When you call matters almost as much as how you call.

Most salespeople fail because they build lazy habits. They call leads at the same time every day, on the same days of the week, and wonder why no one picks up. What they have actually done is train their leads to ignore a specific number at a specific hour.

Predictability kills connection rates.

People's schedules are different today. Hybrid work, kids' sports, commute patterns, back to back meetings. You need to call when your competition is not.

If you rotate your call times correctly, you will reach people your competitors never will.

The Four Call Windows

These are the current best windows based on live data and call connection rates across multiple industries. **Early morning (7:45 to 9:00 AM).** Catch people before work, before meetings start, before the kids take over the morning. High performers tend to pick up early. The inbox is not full yet.

The distractions have not kicked in. **Midday (11:00 AM to 1:00 PM).** Lunch break window. People check their phones between meetings. This is consistently one of the highest connection windows across industries.

Do not skip it. **Late afternoon (4:00 to 6:00 PM).** End of the workday, still at the desk, fewer meetings on the calendar. This window is widely overlooked, which means less competition for the person's attention when you call. **Evening (6:00 to 8:00 PM).** Dinner is done, the kids are winding down. People are finally relaxed enough to actually have a real conversation.

This is especially strong for the gym owner audience where most leads are working parents.

Why You Must Rotate

If you call at 10 AM every day, your number starts to get ignored. People subconsciously recognize patterns. Even if they do not consciously register it, the number becomes familiar in a way that makes it easy to dismiss.

Rotation also gives you data. Certain leads respond better at certain times. Your CRM should be capturing this so you can route future leads smarter.

If someone always picks up in the evening, that is where they live. Stop calling them at noon.

The A B C Rotation Method

This is how you stay disciplined without having to think about it every day.

Split your lead list into three groups. Group A gets called in the early morning window. Group B gets called at midday.

Group C gets called in the evening.

On your second pass, rotate. Group A moves to midday. Group B moves to evening.

Group C moves to early morning. On the third pass, rotate again. Every lead eventually gets hit at every time of day without you manually tracking it.

This keeps your call times fresh and prevents pattern fatigue on both ends.

One note: if your lead volume is under 30, you may not need full rotation yet. Work the windows that fit your schedule and stay consistent. Once your list grows, rotation becomes essential.

Rule of First Week Urgency

If you do not connect with a lead in the first seven days, your chance of reaching them drops by more than half. Speed matters more than most people realize. The moment someone fills out a form, they are at the peak of their interest.

Every hour that passes is interest leaking out.

Your first call should happen within five minutes of the lead coming in if at all possible. If that is not realistic with your schedule, build a system that makes it happen even when you are not available. An AI voice assistant, a team member, a same day callback automation.

Something. Do not let the first seven days slip.

"The person who controls timing controls the connection rate.
When you call is a controllable variable. Use it."

YOUR MOVE

Grab a pen. This is where the work happens.

1. What time do you currently make most of your calls? Is it intentional or is it just habit?

2. Write your three call groups and which time window each gets on the first pass

3. Write your opening script for the qualifying call in your own voice

4. What is your current speed to call? How long after a lead comes in before you dial? What needs to change?

5. Which of the 7 Beliefs do you currently skip or rush? Why?

____

____

____

The Referral System

Your best leads are already in your building

"Your most satisfied customers are your best salespeople."

— Michael LeBoeuf

Your best leads are already in your building. Not the ones walking through the door next week. The ones sweating through a workout right now while you are reading this sentence.

Here is the math most gym owners miss. A referred client closes at roughly three times the rate of a cold lead. They ask fewer questions about price.

They stay longer. They refer more people themselves. And they cost you nothing to acquire.

If that is true, and it is, then why do most gym owners spend ninety percent of their marketing budget on cold ads and almost nothing on a referral system? Because referrals feel passive. They feel like luck.

Something that happens to you if you are good enough.

Referrals are not passive. They are the result of a system. A system that every client walks through whether they know it or not.

Let me show you mine.

"The referral conversation should not feel like an ask. It should feel like a favor you are doing for a client who already wants to help."

Why Most Gym Owners Fail at Referrals

The most common mistake is this. The gym owner waits until a client has been there for six months, feels guilty about not having asked yet, and then drops an awkward question in the middle of a Tuesday workout. Hey, if you know anybody who might be interested... most people freeze right there.

They do not know anybody. Or they do, but they cannot think of one in the moment. Or they feel weird about it.

The second mistake is offering cash for referrals. I know it feels like the obvious move. It is not. When you attach a dollar amount to the ask, you are telling your client that their social capital is worth 50 bucks to you.

That is not how people who love you feel about you. And it is not how you should feel about them.

The third mistake is asking once and never asking again. Referrals are not a one time event. They are a rhythm.

Your best clients should hear the conversation three or four times a year in different forms. Not the same pitch. Different doors into the same room.

When to Ask

There are five moments when a client is at peak willingness to refer someone. If you learn to recognize these moments, you will never have to force the conversation again.

The first is right after a big win. They hit a PR. They dropped a pant size.

Their knee stopped hurting. The moment they tell you about it, their emotional state is high and they want to share it. That is the moment to say something like, you know what is wild, the only reason you got here is because you decided to show up.

If you know one person who needs to make that same decision, I would love to meet them.

The second is at the 30 day mark. By day 30 a new client either feels something changing or they do not. If they feel it, they are ready to talk about it.

Ask them what has been different in the first month. Listen. Then say, who in your life do you think would kill for this same feeling?

The third is when they bring up someone else by name. My husband needs this. My sister has been talking about joining a gym for a year.

My coworker just had knee surgery. Those are the biggest gifts a client can give you and most owners miss them. When they say a name, the right response is, tell me about them.

Not, you should send them my way. Tell me about them.

The fourth is at renewal. If they are signing a new agreement, they are telling you out loud that this was worth it. That is the right moment to say, I want to ask you something.

You just committed to another year with us, which means you already know this works. Who else in your life needs to know?

The fifth is when they do something generous without being asked. They post about the gym on social media. They bring a friend to a party workout.

They leave a review. Every one of those is a moment to say thank you out loud, specifically, and then to ask for one more step. Not in the same breath.

Later the same week.

The Exact Script

Here is the script I use and that I teach my team to use. Memorize it. Then make it sound like you.

Name, can I ask you something. You have had a great couple of months here and I want you to know I see it. You have been showing up, you have been doing the work, and it is paying off.

I am not going to insult you by offering you a discount or a free month for doing what I am about to ask. I am going to ask because I think you care about the people in your life the way I care about the people in mine.

Who is one person in your life right now who is in the same place you were six months ago? Not the whole list. Just one. The one who is on your mind as I say this.

Then you stop talking. Let the silence do its job. Most of the time they will say a name within ten seconds.

Sometimes they will say two. When they give you a name, you do not ask for a phone number on the spot. You do this instead.

That is perfect. Here is what I would love to do. Text them first. Tell them about us. Tell them I am a real person, not a robot, and that I am going to send them a short message in the next day or two.

That way when my name pops up, they already know who I am. Would that be ok?

Now you have a warm introduction instead of a cold message. The client did the hard part and you did not ask them to do anything that felt weird.

"Names come easily when you ask for one. They freeze when you ask for a list."

The Follow Through

Here is where most referral systems die. The client gives you a name. You type it in your notes.

Three days go by. You text the name and you say, hey, I am the owner of the gym your friend trains at. Would you be interested in a free consultation?

The person says no thanks or just does not answer. You blame the referral system and go back to running ads.

That is not the referral system failing. That is you failing the referral.

Within 24 hours of getting a name, your message to that person should look and feel nothing like a cold outreach. It should look like a person who already knows one of their friends and has heard their name in a warm way.

Hey Jordan, this is Tom from the gym. Your buddy Chris mentioned your name to me this morning when we were talking. He said you have been thinking about getting back into it and that you are the kind of person who takes things seriously when you commit.

I do not want to pitch you anything today. I just wanted to introduce myself and tell you that if you ever want to have a real conversation about what would actually work for you, I am here. No pressure at all.

Nine times out of ten that message gets an answer. The one time it does not, you wait seven days and send a check in. Hey Jordan, just circling back.

Still here whenever the timing is right. That is it. That is the entire cadence.

Thanking the Client Who Sent You Somebody

When a client gives you a name that turns into an actual conversation, you say thank you. Publicly if you can. Privately for sure. Not with a gift card.

With a specific thank you that makes them feel seen.

Hey, I just had a great conversation with Jordan. You were right about them. They are the kind of person I love working with.

I want you to know I do not take it lightly that you said my name out loud in your world. It matters. Thank you.

That message costs nothing and it produces more referrals than any paid program ever could. Because the client is not referring for the reward. They are referring because they felt like they were part of something and because you saw it.

The Referral Rhythm on Your Calendar

Put this on your calendar as a recurring task. Every Monday morning, identify three clients to have a referral conversation with that week. Not a pitch. A conversation. Pick people who just had a win, hit their 30 day mark, signed a renewal, or did something generous last week.

Three conversations a week. Twelve conversations a month. Roughly 150 a year.

If half of them give you a name and half of those names turn into a consultation, you are adding 35 to 40 warm conversations a year to your pipeline without spending a dollar on ads.

That is the system. Not luck. Not timing. A repeatable rhythm that runs in the background of your week every week.

YOUR MOVE

Grab a pen. This is where the work happens.

1. Pick three clients this week who are at peak referral moments. Which moment is each of them in, and what will you say to each one?

2. Write your version of the referral script in your own voice. Say it out loud once. Does it sound like you or does it sound like you are reading?

3. Draft the warm introduction message you will send to a referred name. Keep it to five sentences. No pitch.

4. What is your current system for thanking a client who referred someone? If the answer is nothing, what will it be starting this week?

____

____

____

5. Block 30 minutes on your calendar every Monday morning labeled Referral Conversations. Commit to running it every week for the next 90 days.

____

____

____

CHAPTER SEVEN

The Fitness Vision Consultation

Turning a first meeting into a forever client

"People do not buy for logical reasons. They buy for emotional reasons and justify with logic."

— Dan Kennedy

The qualifying call sets the table. The consultation is where you sit down to eat.

By the time someone walks into your gym, you should already know them. Not their age and zip code. You should know what keeps them up at night, what they want to feel like six months from now, what they have tried and why it did not work.

That is the whole point of everything you did on the phone.

When they walk in, the clock does not reset. The relationship continues.

Before They Walk In the Door

Have the consult sheet ready with their name on it. Have a bottle of water waiting. Have the health vision guide printed.

And when they get there, do not start talking about your gym. Start talking about them.

How was the drive? Did you hit any traffic? How long have you been in this area?

Start small, make it human. Ask one question and let them talk. Most people who walk into a gym consultation have not talked to a single person in their life who actually asked them what they want.

You are already ahead of every other gym they have walked into. Before you sit down, ask them: "Is there anything on your mind since we spoke on the phone?" Give them the floor. They might bring up a concern you did not know about.

They might share something that changes the whole direction of your conversation. Either way, you are showing them right from the jump that you listened and you came prepared.

The Goal Question

Once you are sitting, your first question is simple. "I know you mentioned on the phone that you wanted to accomplish this. Now that you are here with me, what is the main thing you want to see happen over the next few months?

Tell me in your own words." You want them to say it again. Not because you forgot. Because hearing it out loud, face to face, makes it real for them.

And you are watching to see if anything has shifted since the phone call. If it has, that is valuable. If it has not, you have just confirmed their commitment.

Keep going from there. By when do they want to see results? What is driving that timeline?

On a scale of one to ten, how serious are they about making this happen? And if they say anything below a ten, ask what it would take to get it there. These questions are not a checklist.

They are a conversation. Think of a doctor who actually gives a damn. Not rushed, not robotic.

Just genuinely trying to understand what is going on with this person.

Health History and Injuries

After you have a solid grasp of their goals, move into health history. Ask about past injuries. Ask about any current limitations. Ask about medications.

Pay attention to how much they share. If someone tells you they have a bad back without any detail, they do not fully trust you yet. If they tell you exactly which disc, when it happened, how it still flares up in the morning, they are in.

You are doing your job. When someone shares a health concern and you respond with knowledge and confidence instead of panic or dismissal, they relax. They stop wondering if you can actually help them and start believing you can.

The Doubt Section

"Tell me about what you have tried before. What worked? What did not? Why do you think it did not stick?" And then let them talk.

Most people who walk through your door have a story of failure sitting on their chest. They tried the big box gym and quit after three weeks. They did a challenge and regained the weight.

They had a trainer who never checked on them. They want to say all of that out loud to someone who is not going to judge them. You are that person.

Let them word vomit everything. Because what they are doing while they are talking is convincing themselves that this time it has to be different. You are not doing the convincing. They are.

The best question in this section is this one: "If you were to try this on your own again, what do you think would get in your way?" Whatever they say, that is the thing you are selling against for the rest of your time together.

The Cost Question

Ask them what happens if nothing changes. Not as a threat. As a reality check.

"What is the cost, for you personally, if six months from now nothing has changed?" Let them sit with it. You are not creating pressure. You are helping them feel the weight of the choice they are already standing in front of.

The Desire Close

Once you have built enough pain and doubt, it is time to hand them the vision. Summarize everything they just told you in their exact words. Then ask: "When you hit that six month mark and you are finally looking in the mirror and feeling the way you want to feel, is there something specific you have been waiting to do?

A trip you want to take? Clothes you want to wear? Something you want to do with your kids?" Let them paint the picture.

That moment is your anchor point for everything that comes next in the sale.

The Support Question

Before you present pricing, ask about their support system. "Does your partner know how much this means to you?" This is not small talk. The support question does two things.

First, it surfaces the spouse objection before it surfaces on its own. Second, it opens the door to bring someone else into If they say yes, the family is on board, you have a green light. If they say no, offer to include the spouse in the consultation or gift them a free trial.

Nine times out of ten, when you ask someone if they want to bring their partner, they say no. They tell you this is for them. And that is exactly the energy you want walking into the close.

YOUR MOVE

Grab a pen. This is where the work happens.

1. What small talk question will you open with to get them talking before the consult begins?

____

____

____

2. Write the cost question in your own voice

____

____

____

3. What is your desire close question, specific to the type of clients you work with?

____

____

____

4. What is your support question, and how do you handle it if they say their partner does not know?

____

____

____

CHAPTER EIGHT

The Art of Building Internal Pressure

How to create urgency without being the one who pushes

"People do not buy for logical reasons. They buy for emotional reasons."

— Zig Ziglar

Most people think closing is about what you say at the end of the call. It is not. The close happens in the middle. It happens when the prospect feels the weight of their own words sitting on their chest and realizes they cannot keep living like this.

That is what building internal pressure is. You are not pushing. You are not convincing.

You are asking the right questions in the right order so the prospect talks themselves into a corner they can only get out of by saying yes.

Let me walk you through exactly how this works.

The Call With Sarah

I am on the phone with a woman named Sarah. She filled out a form on the website. She is a mom.

Two kids. Works full time. She told me she has been "meaning to get back in shape" for a while now.

That phrase right there. Meaning to. That tells me everything. She has been thinking about this for months.

Maybe longer. She has not done anything about it. And every day that goes by she feels a little worse about it. Not worse about her body. Worse about herself.

But I do not say any of that. Not yet.

I ask her what is going on. She tells me she has gained weight. Clothes do not fit.

She is tired all the time. She does not feel like herself anymore.

And here is where most gym owners blow it. They hear that and they jump straight into the pitch. "Oh we can totally help with that, let me tell you about our program." No.

Stop. You have not earned the right to present anything yet. You have not built any pressure. All you have done is let her vent for thirty seconds.

So instead of pitching, I go deeper.

"If you had to put a number on your energy when you wake up, one to ten, where would you say you are at?" She says a three.

A three. Let that land. Do not rush past it. Do not say "oh wow that is low." Just let the silence sit there for a second. Because she just heard herself say out loud that she wakes up every single morning at a three out of ten.

That is heavy. She knows it. You do not need to tell her.

Hell Island

Now I take her somewhere most salespeople are afraid to go. I take her to what I call Hell Island.

This is where you ask the prospect to look forward and imagine nothing changes. You are not being dramatic. You are not trying to scare her.

You are asking a simple honest question.

"And if nothing changes and six to twelve months go by, where do you see yourself?" I drop my voice a little when I say this. I slow down. Because this question matters. This is the one that does the work.

She pauses. And then she says: "Probably heavier. Depressed. More frustrated." Her words. Not mine. I did not tell her she would be depressed.

She told me. And now she is sitting with that picture in her head. She painted it herself. That is the difference between pressure that works and pressure that feels pushy.

When you push, people resist. When they push themselves, they move.

Now I could leave it there. But I do not. Because I know she has kids.

She told me earlier. So I say something like this.

"I get it. And from your kids' perspective, I know if I were them, I would not want my mom feeling like that either." This is not manipulation. This is the truth. Her kids do not want her exhausted and unhappy.

She does not want to be exhausted and unhappy around her kids. I am just connecting the dots she is already been avoiding.

And you can hear it in her voice when it shifts. It gets quieter. Because now this is not about weight loss anymore. It is about who she is as a mother.

It is about the example she is setting. It is about the life she is living versus the life she wants.

"That is internal pressure. And you did not create it. She did.
You just gave her the space to feel it."

Heaven Island

Now I flip it completely.

"Let us go the other direction. If we fast forward six months and everything works out perfectly, what does success look like for you?" She lights up. "Drop 20 pounds. Feel confident again. Have energy to play with my kids." I ask about the kids.

How old are they. What sports they play. She tells me soccer and gymnastics.

And then I ask the question that seals it.

"How do you think they would feel if they started seeing Mom being more active and feeling more like herself again?" She says: "Amazing. I would love that. I would love to feel like me again." Read that sentence back.

I would love to feel like me again. She is not talking about a gym membership. She is talking about her identity.

She is telling me she has lost herself and she wants to come back.

And I still have not pitched anything. I have not mentioned a program. I have not mentioned a price.

I have not mentioned a single feature or benefit or schedule. All I have done is ask questions.

But look at what has happened. She has told me where she is. She has told me where she will be if nothing changes.

She has told me where she wants to be. And she has connected all of it to her kids, her energy, and her identity.

The gap between where she is and where she wants to be is now so wide and so real that she needs a bridge. That bridge is your program. You did not have to sell it.

She is already looking for it.

Why Most Gym Owners Skip This

This is the part most gym owners skip because they are scared of silence. Scared of emotion. Scared of asking hard questions. So they rush to the pitch and wonder why they get objections.

You get objections because you did not build enough internal pressure. When the pressure is right, the prospect closes themselves. Your job at that point is to simply show them the path.

After Sarah tells me how she wants to feel, I do not move on right away. I ask her what she has tried before. Diets. Apps. Programs she could not stick with.

And then I reframe all of it with one sentence.

"So it is not that you are not willing to work. It is that you have been missing structure, accountability, and real support." She says: "Exactly." That one word changes everything. Because now in her mind, the problem is not her.

The problem is that she did not have the right system. And guess what you have.

You did not convince her of that. She convinced herself. You just held up the mirror.

"Internal pressure is not something you create. It is something you reveal. It was already there. You just asked the questions that brought it to the surface."

Hell Island and Heaven Island

Think of two islands. Hell Island is where they are living right now. Overweight, low energy, frustrated, isolated.

They wake up dreading the day. They stand in front of the closet feeling defeated. They say no to things.

That is Hell Island.

Heaven Island is where they want to go. Lean, confident, energized. Keeping up with their kids. Walking into a room and owning it.

Sleeping through the night. Moving without wincing.

Your job is to widen the gap between those two places. Not through manipulation. Through questions that help them feel the contrast clearly. When the gap is wide enough, they feel the pull themselves.

You do not have to push. They jump.

Be Needed, Not Needy

The moment you go into a conversation needing it more than they need you, you lose. Not always that day. But the relationship starts with an imbalance that is very hard to recover from.

Go into every call knowing they need you more than you need them. Not from ego. From service. They are on Hell Island. You know the way to Heaven Island.

You have helped dozens of people make that crossing. They cannot do it alone. That is why they are on the phone with you.

Your energy has to reflect that. Calm. Certain. Curious. When Sarah hears someone on the other end of that phone who is genuinely interested in her situation, not rushing to a pitch, not ticking boxes, actually listening, she relaxes. And people who are relaxed tell you the truth.

And the truth is always where the close lives.

Collecting the Yeses

As you move through the conversation, collect small agreements. Micro commitments that add up.

"You mentioned this has been going on for about three years, is that right?" Yes. "And you have tried a couple of things but nothing has really stuck." Yes. "And what you really want is to feel like yourself again." Yes.

"And you know that doing this on your own is not going to get you there this time." Yes.

By the time you get to the close, they have said yes so many times that no feels inconsistent with everything they just told you. That is not manipulation. That is clarity. You helped them get clear on what is true for them.

The yes is theirs.

YOUR MOVE

1. Describe your ideal client's Hell Island in specific detail. Use a real example from someone you have worked with or spoken to.

____

____

____

2. Write your Hell Island question in your own voice

____

____

____

3. Write your Heaven Island question in your own voice

____

____

____

4. What is the identity statement behind your ideal client's goal? Not the surface goal, the real one underneath it.

____

____

____

5. Write the reframe you will use after someone tells you what they have tried before

____

____

____

Building Your Pricing Model

Simple, profitable, and built to last

"Price is not just a number. It is a statement about who you are and who you serve."

— Dan Kennedy

I am going to tell you about a gym owner named Dave who almost went under because he charged too little.

Dave had a great facility. Good coaches. Strong community. His members loved him. And he was charging $179 a month for small group training because the gym two miles down the road charged $169 and he did not want to lose on price.

Here is what Dave did not realize. He was running 22 sessions a week, coaching most of them himself, paying two part time trainers, covering rent in a decent suburb, and at the end of every month he was taking home less than a public school teacher. Not because the business was failing.

Because the math was broken from the start.

When I sat down with him and we ran the numbers, he went pale. His profit margin was nine percent. One bad month, one trainer quitting, one HVAC repair and he was in the red.

He had built a business that could not survive a single surprise.

We raised his prices to $349 for small group, two sessions a week. He lost four members. He gained eleven new ones in the next 60 days who never flinched at the number.

His margin went from nine percent to twenty eight percent. Same gym. Same coaches. Same community. Different math.

"Dave did not have a sales problem. He had a math problem dressed up as a pricing decision."

The First Rule: Simple Wins

The more options you give people, the harder the decision becomes. And a hard decision is often no decision.

Here is what works: three service types, one or two price points each, and nothing else. When your pricing is this clean, your staff can explain it in thirty seconds. Your clients can make a decision.

And you know exactly what your business is built on.

"Every offer you add is a conversation you have to manage, a system you have to build, and a reason for someone to hesitate instead of commit."

Pick your model. Price it correctly. Sell it confidently. That is the whole game.

The Three Service Types

Small Group Training. Four to eight people. Coached, structured, accountability driven. Minimum floor: $299 per month for two sessions per week.

Below this your margins disappear. **Large Group Training.** Eight or more people. Class based, community focused. Minimum floor: $139 per month for two sessions per week. **One on One Training.** Private coaching.

Highest attention, highest price, lowest volume. Minimum floor: $80 per session on a 24 pack. Below $80 per session you are trading time for money with no leverage.

That is it. Three types. Three floors. You do not need more than this.

Know Your Market

Your floor is the minimum. Your actual price should reflect your local demographic. A gym in Manhattan and a gym in rural Iowa are serving different households at different income levels.

The same $499 per month program that is an easy yes in Scottsdale is a very different conversation in a town where median household income is $45,000.

Before you set your prices, look up the median household income within ten miles of your gym. That number tells you what range you are playing in.

Above $80,000 median income: price at Core or Premium. Between $55,000 and $80,000: Entry to Core is your sweet spot. Below $55,000: stay at or near the floor for small and large group.

The gym offering a $99 product to people who want to spend $399 loses them. The gym offering a $600 program in a $45,000 median income market cannot close it. Price for who is actually in your market.

The Profit Margin Targets

Every fitness business should run at a minimum of twenty percent profit margin. Small group and large group should hit thirty percent. One on one is closer to twenty percent because your time is the entire product and your cost per session is higher.

To calculate your margin, add up every real cost: rent, payroll (including your own hourly rate), utilities, insurance, software, equipment maintenance reserve, marketing, and merchant fees. Divide your net profit by revenue. If you are not hitting twenty percent, either your prices are too low or your costs are too high.

Your hourly rate belongs in that cost calculation. Most gym owners leave themselves out of the math. They pay everyone else first and take whatever is left.

That is not a business. That is a job with worse hours.

A Clean Offer Menu

Five options maximum. That is it. Whatever you offer, whether it is small group, one on one, or a combination, your menu should be clear enough that anyone on your team can explain it in one breath.

If you run small group, your menu might be two times per week, three times per week, and four times per week. Clear pricing for each. If you run one on one, it might be two times per week and three times per week.

If someone wants to come more than that, they buy a bulk package, but that is not on the menu. The menu is what you prescribe to help each person reach their goals.

Next to each option, write out exactly what the client gets beyond the training itself. Accountability check ins. Nutrition guidance. Access to your app. Whatever it is, spell it out.

The value has to be visible.

A prospect should be able to read your entire offer menu in thirty seconds. Your staff should be able to memorize it in five minutes. No one should ever have to calculate anything on the spot.

If you are tempted to add more lines, ask yourself honestly: are you adding options because clients need them, or because you are afraid to say no to a certain type of client? The answer is almost always the second one. And the answer to that is not more offers.

It is better positioning.

"The gym that can explain its pricing in one breath closes more sales. Confusion does not convert. Clarity does."

What Happened to Dave

Six months after we changed his pricing, Dave called me. He said something I will never forget. He said: I finally stopped dreading the first of the month.

That is what correct pricing does. It does not just change your revenue. It changes how you show up.

When you are not worried about making rent, your energy on every call is different. Your patience is longer. Your conviction is real.

You stop discounting because you stop being afraid.

Dave is not a special case. He is what happens when a gym owner stops pricing from fear and starts pricing from math.

YOUR MOVE

Grab a pen. This is where the work happens.

1. What is the median household income within 10 miles of your gym? Look it up right now.

____

____

____

2. Write your three line offer menu with your actual prices.

____

____

____

3. What is your current monthly cost to operate? Include your own hourly rate.

____

____

____

4. What is your current margin? Are you hitting 20% minimum?

____

____

____

5. Is your current pricing based on your market or on what felt comfortable to say? What changes?

____

____

____

Pricing Without Flinching

How your relationship with money shows up in every price you say out loud

---

"The willingness to ask for what you are worth is what separates the successful from everyone else."

— Grant Cardone

The first time I had to say the price out loud, I said it like I was asking for forgiveness. "So, um, it would be around five hundred dollars a month, if that works for you." My voice dropped. My eyes went down.

The prospect did not even push back. They just sensed I was not sure about it either, and that was enough.

The problem was not the price. The problem was my relationship with money.

Your Money Story Is in the Room

Whatever baggage you carry about money does not stay outside when you walk into a consultation. It sits right there with you. If you grew up hearing that asking for money is rude, that belief is in the room.

If you watch people carefully to see if they look like they can afford it before you say the number, that is in the room. If your own bills are tight this month, that is definitely in the room.

You will either price based on your ideal client's value and your delivery, or you will price based on your own bank account. Those are two very different numbers and only one of them builds a business. The goal is to get to a place where you say the price the same way you say your name.

No inflection. No apology. No trailing off. You just say it.

What the Market Actually Supports

Here is something most gym owners do not want to hear. You are almost certainly undercharging.

In the northeast and mid Atlantic region, the market rate for small group personal training is four hundred to seven hundred dollars a month. Midwest suburban markets are similar. These are not aspirational numbers.

These are what the market is already paying at facilities with comparable service When you price yourself at two ninety nine because you are afraid of losing the lead, you are not competing on value. You are competing on fear. And you will attract clients who made their decision based on price, which means they will leave when they find something cheaper.

Price your service based on real math. Small group training should be roughly half the cost of a one on one private session. If you would charge one fifty an hour for private training, your small group rate should sit around fifty dollars per session.

Four to six clients in a small group at fifty dollars each gives you two hundred dollars for that one coaching hour. That is the model.

Presenting the Range

Never state a single number. Present a range.

"Our programs range from two ninety nine to five ninety nine a month, depending on how many times a week you want to come in and how fast you want to reach this goal." The range lets the prospect self select. They hear both ends and naturally gravitate toward what feels manageable. It also removes the shock of a single price.

When you say the range, say it at full voice. Do not drop your volume when you get to the number. Do not add "which I know is a lot" immediately after.

Say the range. Let it sit. Wait for them to respond.

If they say anything below a ten on the priority scale after you share the range, you only ask one thing. "What would have to change for this to be a ten?" Wait for the answer. Do not jump to solutions.

Pricing Front End Offers

A twenty one day jumpstart or a six week challenge is a gateway, not your full offer. Price it accordingly.

If your regular monthly rate is four ninety nine, your front end offer should sit in the two ninety nine to three ninety nine range. Not thirty nine dollars. A thirty nine dollar challenge attracts people who are shopping for free.

A three hundred dollar challenge attracts people who are ready to invest in The only time you can run a deeply discounted front end offer is Black Friday when the goal is list building, not client acquisition. After someone completes a front end offer, the backend conversation is easy. They experienced your coaching, they got results.

Now you are just asking them to keep going at the regular rate.

Leave Your Wallet at the Door

The only time you should think about money during a consultation is when the prospect raises it. Until then, your money story does not belong in the You are not there to decide whether they can afford it. You are there to help them figure out if they want to.

The moment you start looking at someone and thinking "they probably cannot afford this," you have already negotiated against yourself. Let them tell you whether money is the issue.

"People buy Starbucks without thinking about it. They take vacations they did not budget for. People find money for what they want. Your job is to make sure they want it badly enough."

YOUR MOVE

Grab a pen. This is where the work happens.

1. What is your current pricing range? Is it in line with the market data for your area?

____

____

____

2. Practice saying your price range out loud right now at full volume. Write it here

____

____

____

3. What money story do you carry into consultations that works against you?

____

____

____

4. What is your front end offer price and how does it connect to your full monthly rate?

____

____

____

The Monday Morning Scoreboard

The only five numbers that tell you whether your gym is growing

---

"A system without a scoreboard is just activity. Activity is not progress."

— Tom Leonardis Jr.

You now have the system. The calls, the consult, the prescription, the close.

But a system without a scoreboard is just activity. Activity is not progress.

Here are the only five numbers that tell you whether your gym is growing or slowly bleeding out.

Look at them every Monday morning before you do anything else.

Metric 1: Leads

Anyone who expressed interest in the last seven days. Form fills, phone calls, walk ins, DMs, referral names.

Anyone who raised their hand.

Flag if: fewer than 5 per week.

Question to ask yourself: what did we stop doing in the last 30 days that used to bring people in?

Metric 2: Consults Booked

Leads who scheduled an appointment and got on the calendar.

Flag if: booking rate drops below 50 percent.

Question: how long is it taking us to respond after someone reaches out?

Metric 3: Consults Showed

Of everyone who booked, how many actually walked through the door.

Flag if: show rate drops below 70 percent.

Question: what does our confirmation sequence look like between the time someone books and the time they arrive?

Metric 4: New Members

People who signed up and paid this week.

Flag if: close rate drops below 70 percent of people who showed.

Question: am I following a proven consultation framework every single time or am I winging it?

Metric 5: Members Lost

Anyone who cancelled, paused, or ghosted this week.

Flag if: more than 3 members lost in a week, or more than 5 percent of total active members.

Question: at what month of membership are we losing most people and why?

How To Use This

These five numbers will tell you more about your business in five minutes on a Monday morning than any report your software generates.

Know them cold. If one goes wrong, do not panic.

Ask the question underneath it.

The answer is almost always already in your gym. You just stopped looking.

> *"What gets measured gets managed. What gets managed gets better."*

YOUR MOVE

1. Write your leads number from the last 7 days. How does it compare to the flag threshold?

2. Write your current booking rate. If it is below 50 percent, what is the gap?

3. Write your show rate. Walk through what happens between book and arrive and find the leak.

4. Write your close rate on people who showed. Where are you losing them in the consult?

**5. Write the number of members you lost this week and the
month of their membership.**

____

____

____

PART THREE

THE CLOSE

"Every no is just a yes that has not been handled yet."

— Brian Tracy

CHAPTER TEN

The S.A.L.E.S. Framework

Five steps that turn every objection into a close

"Sell the way you would want to be sold to."

— Brian Tracy

THE OBJECTIONS

Every no is just a yes that has not been handled yet.

"The top salespeople in the world are those who handle objections best." — Brian Tracy

Objections Are Not the Enemy

What they really mean and why they are actually good news The first time someone said "I need to think about it" to me, I said "okay, totally understandable" and let them walk out the door. I spent the next hour convincing myself that they were probably going to call back. They did not.

The second time it happened I pushed back a little and it felt awkward and forced. I had not earned the right to push back. I was responding to my own frustration, not their actual need.

It took me a while to realize that what they were really saying had nothing to do with thinking. They were saying "you have not made me feel certain enough to commit." That is different. That is workable.

An Objection Is a Buying Signal

When someone objects, they are still in the conversation. They are still thinking about it. They are still there.

The person who is done with you does not object. They just leave.

What Objections Actually Are

Every objection has a surface, a middle, and a root.

The surface is what they say. It is too expensive. I need to think about it.

My spouse and I need to discuss.

The middle is what they mean. I am not convinced this will work for me. I am overwhelmed and need more time.

I do not feel certain enough to go home and defend this decision.

The root is what actually needs to be addressed. Fear of failure. Fear of commitment. The belief that they will not follow through this time either.

If you respond to the surface, you get nowhere. They dig in. They feel unheard. The conversation dies. If you respond to the root, you close deals.

> *""People do not object to your training. They object to the belief that they will actually follow through this time. And that is where you step in.""*

The people who object the hardest are usually the most serious. They push back because they care. Because they have been burned before.

Because they are smart enough to think before spending money. When someone with real buying power pushes back on you, take it as a compliment.

Think of every objection as a tell me more moment. They are not closing the door. They are inviting you to give them one more reason to walk through it. Accept the invitation.

What You Are Not Doing

Handling an objection is not arguing. It is not convincing someone of something they do not want. It is not wearing them down until they give in out You are guiding someone through the thing that is in their own way.

That thing was there before they walked in your door. It is why they have been sitting on this decision for months. Your job is not to defeat them.

Your job is to help them defeat it.

Now here is the framework. STEP 1

S: Slow Down and Listen

"I need to think about it."

"That is more than I expected."

"My spouse and I need to discuss this."

Cool.

This is not your cue to pounce.

The second someone objects, most salespeople start talking. They defend the price. They list the features.

They offer a discount. They do all of this before the prospect has even finished the sentence. And every word they say makes it worse.

Stop. Breathe. Listen to the actual words. And more importantly, listen to how they say it. Are they frustrated? Scared? Embarrassed? The tone tells you everything about where to go.

This is also where a lot of salespeople lose posture. Their voice goes up. They start shrinking. They apologize for the price before anyone asked them to.

You need to look and sound like the adult in the room. The calmest person in the conversation always leads it.

When you are ready to respond, this is your opening: "Got it. Totally understand. Do you mind if I ask a few quick questions, just to better understand where you are coming from?" That one sentence does three things. It signals that you heard them.

It buys you time to think. And it positions what comes next as a conversation rather than a defense.

What you are listening for: — Is this about money or something deeper? — Have they tried before and it did not work? — Is the spouse objection real or is it a decoy? — Are they scared of committing or scared of failing again? The answers tell you which part of S.A.L.E.S. to lean on hardest. STEP 2

A: Acknowledge and Repeat

Once they finish, repeat the objection back in your own words. Not mockingly. Not robotically. With genuine acknowledgment that you heard them.

"So if I heard you right, it sounds like you are feeling a bit hesitant about the timing, and want to make sure you are making the right move before you commit. Is that fair?" Let them nod. Let them confirm. That moment matters more than people realize.

This step does three things.

It buys trust. The moment someone feels genuinely heard, their defenses come down. Not all the way. But enough. You stop being the salesperson trying to take their money and become the person who actually listened.

It slows the pace down. Fast conversations feel like pressure. Slow conversations feel like partnership.

You are setting the pace and the pace you want is calm and unhurried.

It sets you up to lead. By repeating their objection back, you have framed it as something solvable. You turned their concern into a question.

And questions have answers.

The common mistake here: repeating the surface objection instead of the deeper one. If they say it is too expensive and you say so you are concerned about the price, you just confirmed the surface. Instead try this:

"So it sounds like you want to make sure this is actually going to work before you invest in it. Is that closer to what is on your mind?"

Now you are at the root. They will either confirm it or correct you. Either way you have learned something and the conversation has moved forward. STEP 3

L: Level with Them

This is the neutralizing step. Stay completely level. Make them feel like what they are feeling is completely normal. Then show them that people who felt the same way ended up on the other side of it.

The structure. You do not say these words out loud but the logic follows exactly this sequence:

"Feel. Felt. Found."

"I hear you. A lot of the folks we work with said the same thing at first. They felt unsure, felt like the timing was not perfect, or worried about failing again. But what they found was that this process gave them structure, support, and results faster than they expected.

Because they had someone in their corner this time." Or when they are on the fence about the decision itself:

"I totally get wanting to make the right decision. And if I were in your shoes, I would want to be sure too."

Then pause. Let that land.

"You are not arguing. You are aligning."

The word you are reaching for in this step is neutral. Not defensive. Not eager. Not apologetic. Just calm. Grounded. Like someone who has been in this exact conversation a hundred times and is completely unbothered by where they currently are.

Defensiveness triggers defensiveness. When you stay calm and level, you are modeling the emotional register you want them to move toward. People mirror the energy of the person they are talking to. If you are anxious, they get anxious.

If you are grounded, they start to settle.

"I get it. This is a real decision. Let us just make sure we are thinking about it the right way together."

That phrase, thinking about it the right way together, does something quiet but important. It makes you a partner in the decision. Not a salesperson trying to win it. STEP 4

E: Educate and Equip

Now that they are no longer defensive, you bring in the information. Not everything you know. Just the one specific piece that speaks directly to the root of their concern.

Here is how you set it up: "Let us zoom out for a second. You said earlier you have been trying to figure this out for a while, and what you have been doing has not worked.

You also told me this sounds like exactly what you need." Then you drop the line:

"The investment to finally get you to [their goal] is just [X]."

Then shut up.

Do not explain it. Do not soften it. Do not follow it up with and we also offer.

Say the number and stop talking. The silence after that line is your mic drop moment. Let it do the work.

""You are not selling them on the program. You are selling them on their own goal. That is a different conversation entirely.""

A few more Educate and Equip moments: On the money objection: "You mentioned you have spent money on things before that did not give you results. I hear that. But that money is gone. What we are talking about now is a different kind of investment.

One with accountability built in. One where if you show up, something actually changes. The question is not whether it costs money.

The question is whether it costs more than where you are right now." On the time objection: "I hear you on the schedule. But you also told me you are tired. That you do not have energy for the things that matter.

The reason you do not have energy is the same reason you need this. You are not investing time. You are buying it back." On the spouse objection: "When you go home and say I want to join a gym, that is one conversation.

When you go home and say I talked to someone today about getting my energy back and feeling like myself again, that is a different conversation. How do you think that one goes?" STEP 5

S: Steer It Back to the Close

You have listened. You have acknowledged. You have leveled and educated. Now you bring it home.

They will do one of three things. They will say yes. They will ask more questions.

Or they will throw out another objection. Any of these is fine.

You are ready for all of them.

You redirect with one of these:

"Would that make you feel more confident about getting started?"

"How does that sound to you?"

"Is there anything else holding you back from moving forward today?"

Notice what all three have in common. They are forward facing. They assume momentum. They do not ask whether to move forward.

They ask what is left If they say yes, keep moving. Do not celebrate out loud. Just move.

If they raise another concern, go back to step one. Slow down, listen, acknowledge, level, educate, steer. Every single time. Without frustration.

Without showing that you have been through this twice now. Your posture stays exactly the same on the fifth pass as on the first. If money or logistics are the only things left, now you have earned the right to talk options: — Payment plans — Schedule adjustments — Trial commitment — Looping the partner into a follow up conversation But you do not offer any of those until they are fully bought in on the value.

The moment you jump to options before they believe in the program, you are negotiating from weakness. Hold the frame until they are sold on the why. Then solve the how together.

Add On Tools

Two tools you can drop into any point in the framework when the conversation stalls.

The 1 to 10 Certainty Check

"On a scale from 1 to 10 — 1 being I hate this, 10 being this is exactly what I need — where are you right now on how you feel about the Their number tells you exactly what to do next. — They say 10: "So it is really just the money piece, right?" Now you are talking specifics. Close it. — They say 8 or 9: "What is the difference between an 8 and a 10 for you?" Let them name the gap. Then close it. — They say 7 or below: "What would need to happen for this to feel like a 10?" Now you know exactly where the work is.

This tool is powerful because it gets them to self diagnose. You are not guessing at the objection. You are handing them the microphone and letting them tell you what is still in the way.

Most people have never been asked that question and it cuts through everything.

The Three Choices Close

"Can I be real with you? When someone hesitates at this point, it is usually one of three things. Either you are not totally sure this will actually work for you.

Or you are not sure about me or this gym yet. Or you are already in — you just need to figure out the money part. Which one is you right now?" Simple.

Honest. Gets to the heart of the objection without any guessing.

If they are not sure it will work for them: go back to Educate and Equip with their specific goal.

If they are not sure about you or the gym: address the trust gap head on. Ask what would help them feel more confident. Tell your story. Offer a reference call.

If they need to figure out the money: now you can have a real conversation about what is actually possible. No more dancing around it.

This close works because it treats the person like an adult. You are not manipulating them. You are giving them a framework to understand their own hesitation.

And once they name it, they almost always move.

The Final Word from the Front Lines

If you flinch, they flinch.

But if you lead with conviction, they will follow.

You are not just selling training sessions. You are helping someone rewrite the story they have been stuck in for years. The story that says they will start Monday.

That says they are not the kind of person who follows through. That says something always gets in the way.

This is small group personal training. We are not selling access. We are selling accountability.

Belief. Transformation. The end of I will start And that is worth every dollar they are about to invest. You need to believe that before you can get them to believe it.

Run S.A.L.E.S. on every objection. Not some of them. Every single one. Five steps. In order. Every time. The person on the other end of that conversation does not experience a framework.

They experience someone who actually gave a damn about helping them change their life.

"Lead with conviction. If they feel you believe in this, they will start to believe in it too."

The Objection Playbook

For the full playbook with nine objections and three scripted responses each, turn to the Objection Playbook appendix at the back of this book. Print it. Keep it next to your phone. Use it until you do not need it.

The Noah Text Message

Let me tell you about Noah.

Noah was in my sales training program. He was talented. He had the voice. He had the hunger.

He had everything except one thing. He rushed.

He would fly through the phone call trying to get to the pitch. He wanted the close so badly he was leaping over the parts of the conversation that actually built the close.

I told him to slow down. Get to know the person on the other end. Ask the questions and actually listen to the answers.

And then I told him something specific about frequency.

Stop giving them the choice between two times a week and three times a week. Prescribe three times a week.

Tell them why. Own it. You are the professional. They came to you because they do not know what they need.

If a doctor told you to take a medication twice a day, you would not negotiate it down to once. Sales works the same way when you stop selling and start prescribing.

A few weeks later, I got this text from him.

Hey man, appreciate you for helping me out with the sales convos. The last time we chatted you encouraged me to push everybody to 3x per week and prescribe it to them rather than giving them the choice between two options. Since doing that I have gotten the last 5 out of 6 sign ups to close on 3x per week. Selling 3x per week before this was almost impossible so this is big for us.

Five out of six. At the higher tier. After years of barely getting anyone to three times a week.

Here is what Noah did not realize at first.

He did not become a better salesperson. He became a better diagnostician.

He stopped selling options and started writing prescriptions.

That is the whole chapter in one text message.

YOUR MOVE

1. What is the objection you hear most often? Write it word for word as the prospect says it

2. What is the root of that objection? Not what they say. What they actually mean underneath it

3. Write your Step 1 opening response in your own voice. What do you say after the objection lands?

4. Write your Feel, Felt, Found for your most common objection

5. Write your Educate and Equip moment. Fill in the blanks: "You said earlier you wanted to. And you told me. The investment to get you there is just $."

____

____

____

6. Write your steer back question in your voice

____

____

____

7. Write the Three Choices Close in your own words

____

____

____

CHAPTER ELEVEN

The Close

Moving from yes to started without losing the momentum

"The close is not the end of the sale. It is the beginning of the relationship."

— Grant Cardone

Here is what I need you to understand about the close before I teach you the mechanics of it. The close is not a moment. It is a result.

It is the natural conclusion of everything that came before it. If the qualifying call was done right, if the consultation built the right pressure, if the objections were handled at the root instead of the surface, the close should feel almost anticlimactic. You are not sprinting at the finish line.

You are walking across it.

But sometimes the close does not go the way it is supposed to. Sometimes the prospect nods through the whole conversation and then freezes the moment you ask for the card. Sometimes they give you a wall of no and you have to figure out in real time whether there is a yes still in there.

And sometimes the close does not even happen on the call. Sometimes it happens three days later in a text message.

Let me tell you about one of those.

The Guy Who Said He Did Not Have Time for This

I had a call scheduled with a gym owner. He got on the phone and within about two minutes made it very clear that he had somewhere better to be.

He told me he did not have time for low level conversations.

I want you to understand what had happened at that point. All I had done was ask him to tell me a little bit about his gym, how long he had owned it, and what he was looking to accomplish. That was it. Standard opening. Two sentences. And he had already decided this was beneath him.

In that moment I had two options. I could get defensive or I could get curious. I chose curious.

"I hear you. You want action, not conversation. I respect that. Can I ask you one thing before we wrap up?" He said fine. So I asked him what he felt was the biggest thing holding his gym back right now.

And he answered. Because people who do not want to talk always answer that question. Because it is the one thing they are actually thinking about.

We went back and forth for a few more minutes. He kept saying he did not need any of this, he just needed to take action. And then the call ended.

He did not sign up. He did not book anything. He was gone.

The Text I Sent Out of Spite

I sent him a follow up text.

I want to be honest about where that text came from. It came from a place of certainty. Maybe a little bit of stubbornness too.

Because I knew something about that guy that he had not admitted to himself yet. The fact that he was on a call with me in the first place told me everything. People who are actually taking action are not jumping on discovery calls with coaches.

They are in the gym running their systems.

So I sent him this.

"Hey. I know you are all about action. I respect that. But can I ask you an honest question? Have you actually taken action yet on what needs to happen for you to live the life you want and run the business you know you are capable of?" He said no.

I said: "You want to get on a call again?" He said yes.

> *"One honest question did more than an entire sales call. Because it was the right question, asked from the right place, at the right moment."*

He became a mastermind member. Stayed for two years. And the last I heard, he is coming to our November event.

Not as a current member. Just because he wants to be in the room. That is what happens when you close someone the right way.

They do not just buy the program. They buy into you.

What That Story Is Really About

That story is not about a clever text. It is about three things that you need to carry into every close you ever do.

The first is detachment. I was not desperate when I sent that message. I was not hoping he would say yes so I could hit a number.

I was genuinely curious whether he had followed through on what he said he was going to do. That energy comes through in every word. Needy follow ups feel like chasing.

Confident follow ups feel like coaching.

The second is patience. The close did not happen on the call. It happened three days later.

Most salespeople would have written that guy off the moment he said he did not have time for this. I did not. Because I knew something about where he was even if he did not want to show it.

The third is the honest question. Not a pitch. Not a feature dump. Not a limited time offer.

One honest question about whether he had done the thing he said he was going to do. That question worked because it was true. He had not taken action.

He knew it. He just needed someone willing to say it out loud without flinching.

That is the close. Not a sequence. Not a script. A genuine conversation between someone who has a problem and someone who has a solution, held together by honesty on both sides.

The Prescription Close

Most gyms present their prices the same way. They slide a laminated card across the table, point to the most popular tier, and say something like most of our members go with option two.

That is not a sales process. That is a menu. And a menu makes you a commodity.

When someone sits down with you, they did not come to compare your options. They came because they have a problem and they believe you might be the person who can fix it. Your job in that moment is not to present options.

Your job is to write a prescription.

A doctor does not hand you a list of medications and say which one is most popular. They ask questions, listen to your answers, make a diagnosis, and tell you exactly what you need. You trust the prescription because it was made specifically for you.

That is exactly how you present your program. No price sheet. No pointing at a menu. A written prescription based on the consultation you just had, delivered as the expert who listened and now knows exactly what this person needs.

How It Works in the Room

By the time you get to the prescription, you have already done the consultation. You know their goal. You know their timeline.

You know what their Hell Island looks like. All of that is the raw material for the prescription.

Here is what it sounds like. Sarah wants to lose thirty pounds before her July trip. She told you she hates getting dressed in the morning because nothing feels right.

You do not pull out a price card. You lean forward and say:

"Okay, so based on everything you just told me, here is what I want to do for you."

Then you walk her through it. Every element tied directly back to something she told you.

"You want to lose thirty pounds before your July trip. That is four months. To hit that in that window, you are going to need to come in at minimum three times per week. Here is why that matters. I am only going to see you for about two hours out of the 168 hours in your week. Two hours is not enough for me to move the needle on its own. Three sessions gives us the training volume we need to actually get you there in the time frame you told me."

Notice what just happened. You did not state the frequency and then ask if that works. You explained it by connecting it directly to her goal and her timeline.

It is not a recommendation. It is a prescription.

Then you layer in the full picture:

"Here is what your week looks like. Three small group sessions for your strength and coaching work. As part of this, you also get two large group classes included. That is

your cardio, your caloric burn throughout the week. So right now you are looking at five days of training if you want it."

"We are also going to point you in the right direction on nutrition. We do not hand you a rigid meal plan, but we are going to make sure you understand what you should be eating and when, because training three times a week without any attention to what you eat will slow everything down."

"You also get access to our private member group. That is where you are going to connect with other people going through the same thing. It matters more than you think."

By the time you finish walking through the prescription, she has not heard a price yet. But she has heard her goal repeated back to her. She has heard a specific plan designed around exactly what she told you she needed.

"When they hear their own goal inside your solution, the price becomes part of the plan rather than a barrier to it."

Then You Say the Number

After you have walked through everything, you say the price. Not before. Not in the middle. After.

You say it the same way you say your name. Flat. Certain. No inflection. No apology.

"To make all of this happen, what I am going to need from you is the card you want on file. Everything is month to month. We do not lock you into contracts because we do not need to. Our members stay an average of fifteen to eighteen months. Some of them have been with us for seven years. We stay month to month because we trust what we do. And all I need right now is to get the card on file and get you set up on the app so you can start scheduling."

That is the close. The prescription was the presentation. The card is the implementation.

When you say we stay month to month because we trust what we do, you are making a confidence statement. You are telling them you are so certain about your product that you do not need a contract to keep them. That removes risk. And when risk is removed, hesitation goes with it.

Why There Is No Price Sheet

The price sheet does three things, all of them bad.

First, it makes you look the same as every other gym. When you pull one out, you instantly become a commodity. The prospect starts comparing your prices to the gym down the street.

Second, it hands control of the conversation to them. The moment they see a list of options, they start choosing. They almost always choose the cheapest one or start asking why one costs more than another.

Now you are defending pricing instead of building value.

Third, it tells them you did not listen. A price sheet says here are our options. A prescription says here is what you need.

One is a menu. The other is a diagnosis.

The prescription model is built on everything you learned in the consultation. The goal, the timeline, the specific pain, the identity shift they described. You take all of that and build a program specifically for them.

Then you present it. Then you say the number.

The Close Sequence

With that said, here is the actual mechanics of what the close looks like when you are in the room or on the call and everything has gone well.

"Alright, here is what we are going to do. I am going to need your card to put on file. Then we are going to open your phone, download the app, and schedule your first session.

Ready?" Three things. Card, app, session. In order. Every time. When you do it the same way every time, you stop thinking about the words and start paying attention to the person in front of you.

When They Hesitate at the Card

Sometimes someone will say yes in their heart and then freeze the moment you ask for the card. This is not a new objection. This is old habit.

They have been on Hell Island so long that even when they want to leave, the departure feels scary.

You handle it with one of three safety nets. **Safety net one:** Loop back to the goal. "Let me just confirm one thing. You still want to reach this goal, right?

Okay. Then this is step one. There is no step one without this." Keep moving. **Safety net two:** Take the urgency off the commitment but not the direction. "No rush on anything else.

Just this first step. You are month to month so the only thing you are committing to is starting." Keep moving. **Safety net three:** Bring back the cost. "Listen. Eight out of ten people who walk out of here without getting started come back to me six months later having gained more weight and feeling worse.

I do not want that to be your story. You are already in the right place. Let us keep going." Use one.

Not all three. And return immediately to the close after whichever one you use. Do not circle back through the objection again. The person who hesitates at the card is not saying no.

They are saying they need one more reason to say yes. Give them that one reason and move.

YOUR MOVE

1. Think of a close that went wrong. What happened and at what moment did it slip away?

____

____

____

2. Write your exact close sequence in your own words

____

____

____

3. Which safety net phrase feels most natural to you? Write it here

____

____

____

4. Write the honest follow up text you would send to a prospect who left without committing

____

____

____

5. What is the one thing you are going to stop doing at the close that is costing you deals right now?

____

____

____

6. What is your plan if they freeze right at the card step?

____

____

____

CHAPTER TWELVE

Sold... Now What?

The first thirty days determine the next twelve months

"The sale is not the end of the relationship. It is the beginning of the real one."

— Harvey Mackay

The moment someone swipes their card, your job as a salesperson is done and your job as a coach begins. And the transition has to be seamless.

Most gyms drop the ball here. They close the sale, send a welcome email, and then see the person at their first session as if they have never met. All that momentum from the consultation disappears.

The client starts fresh with a trainer who does not know their story. That gap kills retention.

The First Forty Eight Hours

Within twenty four hours of the close, the new client should receive a personal message from you. Not automated. From you. Referencing something specific from the consultation. Their goal. Their why. Their anchor.

"Hey, I just wanted to tell you I am fired up for you. What you shared with me today about wanting to show up differently for your kids, that stuck with me.

We are going to make this happen. Your first session is Monday. Coach Chris knows you are coming and knows your story.

See you there." That message does three things. It shows them you listened. It reminds them why they said yes.

And it sets the expectation that they are walking into a relationship, not a transaction.

The Goal Sheet Handoff

Everything you gathered during the qualifying call and the consultation needs to be documented and handed to the coaching team before that first session. The coach who trains this person for the first time should know their primary goal, the specific pain that drove them to join, their injury history, and any personal details that help build the connection. If you do not have a formal handoff process, build one.

A simple one page intake sheet that travels with the client from the sales conversation into the coaching relationship. The coach should be able to walk up to a new client and say "I know you want to lose twenty pounds, I know your back has been giving you trouble, and I know your daughter's wedding is in May." That kind of greeting turns a new client into a lifer.

The First Session Experience

If you can be physically present for a new client's first session, be there. Even if it is just to walk them in, introduce them to the coach, and say "I told you you were going to love this." Your presence in that first session reinforces everything you built during the sales process.

And send them something before they come. A guide to their first session. What to wear. When to arrive. What to expect. Take the unknowns off the table so all they have to think about is showing up.

Day Fourteen Check In

Two weeks in, check on them. Not the coach. You. A personal message.

"Hey, two weeks in. How are you feeling? I want to make sure
you are getting what you came here for. Any wins to report?"

This is not a sales call. You are showing them that you are still invested in their success. The close did not end the relationship.

It deepened it. A client who tells you something feels off two weeks in is giving you the chance to keep them. A client who lets something fester for three months and then cancels gives you nothing.

Day Thirty Review

At the thirty day mark, schedule a brief check in to review progress against the original goal. Pull out the notes from the consultation. Compare where they are to where they said they wanted to be.

In most cases, they will not have hit the goal yet. That is fine. That is expected. What you are doing is showing them you remember, you care, and you have a plan. And it is also when you plant the seed for the first upsell conversation.

YOUR MOVE

Grab a pen. This is where the work happens.

1. What does your current new client handoff look like? Where are the gaps?

____

____

2. Write the personal message you will send within 24 hours of a new client's close

____

____

3. What does your day 14 check in message sound like?

____

____

4. What information from the consultation currently gets lost before the first session?

____

____

CHAPTER THIRTEEN

Reactivation and Upsells

The money your gym is already sitting on top of

"Your existing customers are your most underutilized revenue opportunity."

— Sabri Suby

I want to tell you about a text message that made us $14,000 in a week.

It was September. The summer had been slow the way summers always are. People go on vacation. They fall off. They say they will come back after Labor Day and then Labor Day comes and goes and they do not.

We had a list of about 40 people. Past clients, expired trials, leads who had come in for a consult and never signed up. People who at some point raised their hand and said yes, I want this, and then life got in the way.

I sat down one Tuesday morning and sent each of them a text. Not a promotion. Not a special offer. Not a we miss you email blast.

A personal message. One at a time.

> *"Hey, it has been a while since we talked. Your name came up*
> *in a conversation here the other day. Just wanted to reach out*
> *and see how things are going."*

Seventeen people responded. Out of those seventeen, eleven booked a call. Out of those eleven, eight came back. Average monthly rate of $449.

That is over $3,500 in new monthly recurring revenue from one morning of text messages to people who already knew us.

Every gym is sitting on a list like that. Most gyms never touch it.

The Three Lists

Every gym has three lists. Active members. Past clients and trials that did not convert. Cold leads. Most gyms only talk to the first one.

And most of the time talking to them means sending the same newsletter to everyone and hoping someone buys.

The second list — past clients and expired trials — is the most valuable list you own. These people already walked through your door. They already felt your energy.

They already know your coaches by name. The only reason they left is because something in their life shifted and nobody reached out to pull them back.

That is not a lost client. That is an open conversation that went quiet. Your job is to restart it.

The Reactivation Campaign

Run a reactivation campaign once a quarter, minimum. Not an email blast. Not a coupon code.

A human being sending a human message to another human being.

Here is what works. Three separate texts. Short. Personal. No novel.

Text one: "Hey, it has been a while since we talked. Your name came up in a conversation here the other day. Just wanted to reach out and see how things are going." Send. Wait.

Text two (if no response after 48 hours): "Hey, we have been getting some really great results in the program lately and honestly we have missed having you here. Would you be open to a quick call this week?" Send. Wait.

Text three (if still no response): "Last thing from me. If you ever want to come back, the door is always open. No pressure. Just wanted you to know." Send. Done.

The goal is not to sell them in the text. The goal is to get them to respond. A response is a conversation.

A conversation can lead anywhere.

Timing the Reactivation

Align your campaigns with natural transition points. Back to school. New Year. Spring. The week after Labor Day. These are the moments when people feel the pull to restart.

If most of your client base has kids, the school year calendar is your reactivation calendar. Warm up your list two weeks before school starts so that when the fall promotions kick in, the people on your list are already engaged.

"Warm list plus compelling offer beats cold list plus the same

offer every single time."

The Upsell Conversation

I watched a gym owner named Jen do something that I now teach to every owner I work with.

She had a client, Marcus, who had been coming twice a week for about four months. Consistent. Never missed. Clearly loved being there. One day after his session she walked over and said: "Hey, your coaches have been telling me great things about your progress.

I have a question for you. What do you think your results would look like if you were coming in three times a week instead of two?"

Marcus said he had actually been thinking about it. She said: "I want to give you three times a week on me for the next thirty days. After that, we talk about keeping it that way."

He upgraded the next month. No pitch. No pressure. She gave him the experience first and let the results sell the upgrade.

That is how upsells work in fitness. You are not asking someone to spend more money. You are giving them a taste of what more commitment actually feels like.

The conversation writes itself after that.

Upgrade Paths by Model

If your model is large group, the upsell is small group. Not more large group. The intimacy and the coaching attention that comes with small group is your differentiator and it is worth more money.

If your model is small group, the upsell is increased frequency. Move two day clients to three days. Move three day clients to four days.

Tie the upgrade to their goal and their progress data.

If you offer nutrition coaching, personal training packs, or any kind of wellness service alongside your main training product, those are natural add ons once a client is established. Plant the seed at thirty days. Offer it at sixty.

The Power of the Gift

The most underused tool in client retention is the gift. Not a coupon. Not a discount code. A gift. Something you give without an ask attached.

A free week of extra sessions. A tub of protein with a handwritten note. A personalized travel workout before their vacation.

These things cost you almost nothing and they create the kind of goodwill that money cannot buy.

I watched a gym give every member a small gift bag on their one year anniversary. A branded shaker, a thank you card signed by the coaches, and a framed before and after photo. The cost was maybe fifteen dollars per member.

Three of those members posted it on Instagram that night. Two of those posts brought in new leads the next week.

"The gym that knows your name, remembers your goals, celebrates your wins, and occasionally shows up with something unexpected is the gym nobody wants to leave."

YOUR MOVE

Grab a pen. This is where the work happens.

1. Write the names of five past clients or trials you will send a reactivation text to this week.

____

____

____

2. Write the exact reactivation text you will send to one of them. Make it personal.

____

____

____

3. Which current client is most ready for an upsell? What will you offer and how will you frame it?

____

____

____

4. What gift could you start giving to clients at the one year mark? What would it cost per person?

____

____

____

CHAPTER FOURTEEN

Sell by Chat

How to convert leads without ever picking up the phone

"Silence is the loudest form of negotiation."

— Chris Voss

That person is sitting in your DMs right now waiting for a real human to say something real to them.

Most gym owners never say anything. They run the automated follow up sequence, watch it bounce off with no response, and write the lead off. Meanwhile that person is still watching every post, still thinking about it, still one good conversation away from becoming a client.

Sell by chat is how you have that conversation. Not to replace the phone call. To get to it.

The message is the bridge. The call is the close.

This chapter is going to give you the full playbook: how to open a chat conversation without sounding like a robot, how to qualify someone in three text messages, how Instagram DMs and Facebook Messenger and SMS each play differently, and how to know when to push for the call.

Before I give you the scripts, I want to credit the person who built the foundation of what I am about to show you. The framework I am about to show you is adapted from Dan Martell's Sell by Chat Playbook from his book Buy Back Your Time. Credit where it is due — the foundation is his.

What I have done is translate it into the world of gym ownership.

The O Q C Framework: Open, Qualify, Close

Here is the O Q C framework. Three moves. In order. In every conversation. I am going to walk you through what each step looks like when you are a gym owner talking to a local person who might want to change their life.

O — Open: Start a real conversation. Sound like a human.

Q — Qualify: Find out where they are and whether they are a fit.

C — Close: Book the next step. A consult, a call, a visit.

O — Open: Sound Like You

The open is not a pitch. It is not a soft pitch either. It is a gym owner who noticed someone and decided to say hello.

The test is this: if your gym's front desk person sent this message to a neighbor they ran into at the grocery store, would it feel weird? If yes, it is too salesy. If no, you are in the right place.

Here is what an open looks like for a gym owner: "Hey [name]. This is [you] from [gym name]. I noticed you have been following us for a while and just wanted to reach out personally.

How are things going with your fitness right now?" That is it. No list of what you offer. No special promotion. No tour booking link.

Just a person reaching out to another person to ask how they are More opens that work for a gym owner:

Here is how I teach gym owners to open on Instagram. When someone new follows your page, you send one message. "Hey, thanks for the follow.

Are you here for content or are you looking for help with your health and fitness?" That is it. One question. It probes without pushing. If they say content, great — you just started a relationship.

If they say they are looking for help, you are already qualifying.

When someone likes or comments on a specific post, that is your signal. Message them. "Hey, I saw you liked our post about [topic]. Did you go through something similar, or are you working towards something right now?" Bring that approach to every engagement.

Every like is someone raising their hand halfway. Your job is to notice it and say hello.

"Hey, saw you commented on our post about [topic]. That resonated with a lot of people. Are you currently working with anyone on that?"

"Hey, this is [name] from [gym]. You filled out our form a little while back. Life got busy, totally get it.

Just wanted to personally check in. Did I catch you at an okay time?" What you are listening for when they respond: are they talking? Even a short answer tells you there is a door open.

Work with whatever they give you.

Q — Qualify: Find Out Where They Are

Once they respond, your one job is to understand what is actually going on for them. Not to sell. Not to tell them about your programs. Just to Ask the question that opens the door:

"What made you decide to follow the gym? Is there something specific you have been thinking about working on?"

Or if they reached out after a post about energy or weight loss: "What has been going on? How long has this been on your mind?" Then stop talking. Let them type. The more they share, the more invested they become.

And the more they tell you, the better you understand which version of your program is actually right for them.

Qualify questions that work in the gym context: — How long has this been something you have been thinking about? — What have you tried before and what happened? — What does your schedule look like right now? — Are you trying to figure this out on your own or are you open to getting some support? That last question is the hinge. Their answer tells you everything about whether to move to the close or keep qualifying.

C — Close: Book the Specific Next Step

Once you understand where they are and what they want, you make a specific move. Not "we should talk sometime." A specific option.

"Based on what you just shared, I really think you would be a strong fit for what we do here. The best next step is to come in and sit down with me for about thirty minutes so I can actually see where you are starting from. I have Tuesday at nine in the morning or Thursday at six in the evening open this week.

Which one works better?" Two options. Not an open calendar. Two specific times. Same principle as the qualifying call close from earlier in the book.

If they are not ready to come in, your close is the phone call: "Would it be okay if I gave you a quick call this week? Ten minutes. I just want to make sure I actually understand what you are dealing with before I suggest anything. What number is best for you?" Chat gets you the call.

The call gets you the consult. The consult closes the new member. Know which step you are on and only play for that step.

PSL: The Content That Fills Your Inbox

Before you can message people, you need people reaching out to you. And before they reach out, they need a reason to. That reason is your content.

Here is a content approach for your Instagram or Facebook posts: Pain (name a specific problem), Solution (show how you solve it),

Launch (tell them what to do next). Comment a word. DM you. Send them a QR code. Whatever makes it easy.

Here is how it translates directly to a gym owner posting on Instagram or Facebook: PSL — Pain, Solution, Launch (for gym owners) Pain: Name the exact thing your ideal member is feeling right now. Solution: Show them there is a way out. Not your program. A shift in thinking.

Launch: Tell them exactly what to do next. Comment a word. DM you.

A real example for a local gym posting to working parents: Pain: "If you have been waking up exhausted, skipping workouts because life keeps getting in the way, and telling yourself you will start Monday for the last six months... this is for you." Solution: "The problem is not your schedule and it is not your discipline. The problem is that you have been trying to do it alone. The people who make it work have one thing different: accountability." Launch: "Comment the word YES below and I will send you a free breakdown of how our members fit training into a schedule just like yours." Everyone who comments YES is a warm lead.

You message them. The O Q C starts. You have thirty seconds of their attention and a specific reason to This is not about going viral. It is about getting the right few people to raise their hand.

A gym selling a five hundred dollar a month small group program does not need thousands of comments. It needs ten people who are genuinely interested. PSL content gets you those ten.

Then you work them.

"The post gets them interested. The conversation gets them in the door. The consult closes the deal."

How Each Platform Plays Differently

Instagram DMs, Facebook Messenger, and text message are not the same conversation. The person on the other end has different expectations on each one.

Match the platform or you will lose them.

Instagram DMs

Instagram leads come warm. Ninety percent of the time, the person who DMs you on Instagram just finished watching your reel, or they commented on a post and you messaged them because of that. They know who you are. They picked you.

That warmth is your biggest asset. Use it. Reference what they engaged with.

"Hey, glad you reached out. What was it about that post that

hit home for you?"

Keep messages short on Instagram. Two or three sentences per message. Shorter back and forth feels more human than big paragraphs.

Think about how you text a friend and write like that.

Look at their profile before you respond. If they have kids, mention yours. If they posted about running a race, acknowledge it.

Instagram gives you context that text and Facebook do not always give you. Use thirty seconds to look, then respond like someone who actually paid attention. "Saw you have a little one at home.

That makes getting to the gym feel like a whole project. Is that part of what has been making this hard?" Speed matters on Instagram more than anywhere else. The window after someone engages with your content is short.

Respond within fifteen minutes if you can. Within an hour at the most. Slow responses on Instagram feel like you are not really paying attention.

Facebook Messenger

Facebook is where your slightly older audience lives. The people messaging you through Facebook are often coming from a more deliberate place. They saw something in a community group, or they have been following your page for a while, or they clicked through from a Facebook ad.

They have been thinking about this longer than the person who saw your reel twenty minutes ago.

Facebook conversations can be a little longer than Instagram conversations. A slightly fuller response is acceptable because the platform trains people to expect it. This is where a voice note can absolutely separate you from every other gym in the area.

A thirty second voice note on Facebook Messenger is almost guaranteed to get a response. Nobody does it. It sounds like a real human instantly. Record it like you are leaving a message for a friend, not presenting to a room.

What a Facebook open looks like: "Hey [name], I saw your comment in the group and it really resonated with me. I wanted to reach out personally. What has been going on with your fitness lately?" Facebook groups are where this gets especially powerful for gym owners.

If you are active in your local parents group, your neighborhood page, any community group, the DMs you get from those interactions have built in context and trust. You are not a stranger. You are the gym owner from the Comment on posts where someone mentions struggling with energy, wanting to lose weight, feeling out of shape.

Do not pitch in the comments. Say something real and genuine. Then the DM becomes a continuation, not a cold open.

SMS and Text

Text is the most personal of the three. When someone gave you their phone number, whether through a form or a QR code or in person, they extended a level of trust that a social follow does not. Protect that trust. Do not burn it with a sequence that sounds like a car dealership.

The number one mistake gym owners make with text leads: sounding automated. People know the difference. They have felt it a hundred times from other businesses.

The moment they feel the automation, the lead is dead.

Text rules that keep the trust alive:

Three lines maximum per text. Shorter is more human. No links in the first three messages.

Links are what bots send. Use their name once, early. Just once. More than that feels scripted.

A typo or two is fine. Perfect grammar on a text feels like a press release. Send your reply ten to twenty minutes after they respond.

Instant responses at 2 AM feel automated. Human responses have a rhythm.

Here is what the O Q C looks like over text for a gym owner:

Open:

"Hey [name], this is [your name] from [gym]. You filled out our form earlier. Wanted to personally reach out.

Did I catch you at an okay

Qualify:

"What made you look into us right now? What has been going on?"

Let them answer. Ask one more question. Then close:

"Based on what you just told me, I really think we can help. What does your week look like? I have a couple of spots to sit down with someone for about thirty minutes this week." The double text is a text specific move that gets attention without being aggressive.

If someone goes quiet after your first message, send two short messages close together instead of one long follow up:

"Hey, wanted to make sure this did not get buried in your messages."

Ten seconds. Then:

"Still curious to hear what you have been dealing with."

Two short messages. It reads like a real person remembered to check in, not a CRM firing a sequence. Works on Instagram and Facebook too but it was built for text.

What Chat Cannot Replace

Chat gets you in the conversation. The consultation closes the member. Do not confuse the two.

You cannot run the full qualifying call over text. You cannot build the internal pressure, handle the objections properly, and close a five hundred dollar a month program in a DM thread. The nuance is not there.

The silence does not work the same way. The emotional read is gone.

Your only goal in a chat conversation is to get them on the phone or into your gym. That is the finish line. Every message you send is in service of that one thing.

When you lose sight of that and start trying to sell the program in the thread, you lose the lead.

The exception is a lower ticket entry offer. If you are running a four week challenge at a hundred and fifty dollars or a free week trial, you can sometimes close that in the DMs after a qualify. But the higher the investment, the more a real conversation matters.

Your flagship program needs the consultation. The chat just gets them there.

"Chat is social. The call is sales. Know which one you are in at every moment."

Making This a Daily Habit

The reason most gym owners never build a chat selling habit is the same reason they never build any selling habit: they wait until they need clients to start doing the activity. And by then it is desperate energy and desperate energy shows.

Build the habit now. Every single day, do these three things: reply to every DM and comment within one hour during business hours, message five people who engaged with your content in the last forty eight hours, and post one piece of PSL content per day. Pain, solution, call to action.

Three things. Every day. The people you message today are not joining today. They are joining in three to six weeks when the conversation has had time to build. Which means the clients you want in six weeks need you to start messaging now.

Here is the reality: most gym owners think they have a lead problem. But look at the people who already follow you, already watch your content, already know who you are, and have never once been reached out to.

Your next ten members are probably already watching your page. They are just waiting for you to say something.

"The fastest way to more clients is not a better ad. It is saying hello to the people who are already watching."

YOUR MOVE

Grab a pen. This is where the work happens.

1. Write your Instagram open for someone who just followed your gym. Sound like yourself

____

____

____

2. Write your Facebook Messenger open for someone who commented on one of your posts

____

____

____

3. Write your text open for a new form submission

____

____

____

4. Write your three best qualify questions for a local gym prospect

____

____

____

5. Write your close. Two time options, specific, in your voice

____

____

____

6. Write a PSL post for your gym. Pain, Solution, Launch in three short paragraphs

____

____

____

7. Which platform are you most underusing right now and what is your plan for it this week

____

____

____

The Role Play Chapter

How to practice until it is automatic

"Amateurs practice until they get it right. Professionals practice until they cannot get it wrong."

— Dan Kennedy

How Role Play Works in the sales training program

In the sales training program, I had people call me as the prospect and I went through the whole call live. I made mistakes on purpose. I pushed back. I gave them money objections and spouse objections and gym jumper energy and they had to figure out where to go.

The most important thing I observed was this: most people knew the answer. They had absorbed the frameworks. But when I said "it is too expensive" out loud and they had to respond in real time, they froze.

Or they rushed. Or they answered the surface and ignored the root. That gap between knowing it and doing it, that is what role play closes.

Three Role Play Scenarios

Scenario 1: The Qualifying Call

One person plays the prospect. The prospect is forty two years old, has two kids, has tried a gym twice before and quit both times, and is mainly worried about the cost. Their real why is being able to keep up with their kids without hurting themselves.

The salesperson runs the full qualifying call: opener, seven beliefs, money priority question, support question, three question close. After the call, the observer writes down: What built the most trust?

What moment created the most internal pressure? Where did the salesperson rush? What question was never asked?

Scenario 2: The Consultation Close

The same prospect has now come in for the consultation. They went through the full vision process. They are interested but hesitant.

At the close, they say: "I like it but I really do need to think about it. Can I have a day or two?" The salesperson handles the hesitation using one of the three safety nets, returns immediately to the close, and books the session.

After the scenario, discuss: Which safety net was used? Did it work? Why or why not?

Scenario 3: The Objection Stack

The prospect says: "It is more expensive than I expected." The salesperson handles it. Then the prospect says: "I also just feel like my schedule is really unpredictable." The salesperson recognizes the stack and calls it directly. Debrief: Did the salesperson go back to S.A.L.E.S. for each objection or did they address both at once?

Your Role Play Reflection Sheet

After every role play, fill this out. Not after three role plays. After every single one.

This is where the learning lives.

YOUR MOVE

Grab a pen. This is where the work happens.

1. What part of the conversation built the most trust?

2. Which framework did you lean on most? (S.A.L.E.S., Feel Felt Found, Three Choice Close, Certainty Scale)

3. Did you use the one to ten scale? What did it reveal?

Onboarding a Salesperson in 90 Days

How to build a sales seat that does not fall apart in month three

---

"Build a system that runs without you, or you have built yourself a job."

— Sabri Suby

At some point, you are going to want to get out of the sales seat. Or you are going to grow past the point where you can do all the calls yourself. Either way, you will need to hand this off to someone.

And when you do, you are going to find out very quickly whether your sales process exists inside your head or on paper. If it exists in your head, your new hire is going to have a rough first month. If you built systems and documented everything, they are going to thrive.

What to Look for Before You Hire

The best salespeople in fitness are not always the most extroverted. They are the most curious. They ask good questions.

They actually listen to the answer. They care about the person they are talking to, not just about the close.

Before you hire someone into a sales role, role play with them. Tell them you are going to play a prospect and ask them to qualify you. Give them a real scenario.

See what they do with silence. See how they handle it when you push back. See if they can slow down and dig or if they immediately try to solve.

Technical skills can be taught. Genuine curiosity and care for other people is much harder to build from scratch.

Days 1 Through 30: Learn the Language

In the first thirty days, the new salesperson should not be taking solo calls. They should be listening. Sitting next to you or on calls with you while you work.

Watching how you open a call. Watching how you navigate a tough objection. Watching how you close.

They should have a copy of this book. They should be doing the Your Move sections at the end of every chapter and the role play scenarios from Bonus One multiple times a week. By day thirty, they should be able to articulate the seven beliefs, walk through the consultation framework, and handle the five most common objections in a role play setting.

Days 31 Through 60: Supervised Reps

In month two, they start taking calls with you present. Either you are sitting next to them or the call is being recorded and reviewed together after.

After every call, run the reflection sheet from Bonus One together.

This is the period where habits form. The good ones and the bad ones. Your job is to catch the bad ones before they calcify.

The most common bad habits I see in new salespeople: rushing through the pain questions, not using silence effectively, going to the solution before the prospect has fully felt the problem, and softening their voice on the price. Catch those four and you are ahead of ninety percent of fitness salespeople.

Days 61 Through 90: Independence with Review

By month three, they are running their own calls independently. You are doing a weekly call review together, going through recordings and discussing what worked and what to adjust.

At the ninety day mark, pull up their close rate data. What percentage of qualified consults are converting? What percentage of calls are converting to consults?

Where is the leak in the pipeline? If they are closing at sixty percent or better by ninety days, you have a salesperson. If they are below fifty percent, you have more work to do.

The Sales Journal as Onboarding Tool

The Your Move sections, the call script in Appendix A, the objection playbook in Appendix B, every consultation sheet, every framework in this book, that is your onboarding tool. Not a slideshow. Not a one pager. The whole thing.

A new hire who goes through every page of that journal and does every exercise and fills out every worksheet will have a foundation that most salespeople in this industry never get. You are not just giving them a job. You are giving them a playbook.

What You Cannot Delegate

You can delegate the calls. You can delegate the consultations. You can even delegate the close over time.

What you cannot delegate is the culture. The standard. The belief that this work matters and deserves to be done with full care and full attention.

Your salesperson will mirror what you model. If you are sloppy with follow up, they will be sloppy with follow up. If you take shortcuts in the consultation, they will take shortcuts.

If you show them through your own behavior that every lead deserves a real conversation and every prospect deserves to be heard, that standard becomes the culture.

That is the thing you protect most carefully when you build a sales team. Not the scripts.

"The standard."

YOUR MOVE

1. What does your current sales documentation look like? What is missing?

____

____

____

2. What are the three things you need to capture in writing before you can hand this off?

____

____

____

3. What role play scenario would you use to vet a potential new hire?

____

____

____

4. What is the one standard you will protect above everything else as your team grows?

____

____

____

One More Thing Before You Go

Because the reps are what close the deals

"The secret of getting ahead is getting started."

— Mark Twain

I want to go back to Hailey and Hudson for a second.

A few weeks ago we were sitting at the kitchen table. Hailey had a blue ice pop.

She said look at my ice pop. Then she said smell it, it smells like blueberries.

Then, without asking, she stuck it in my mouth and said does not that taste good?

Hudson was at the same table eating his own ice pop out of a bowl. Laughing at himself for taking it in and out.

Kristin was at the counter watching the whole thing.

Here is the thing I did not realize in the moment.

My three year old daughter just ran a perfect sales sequence on me.

Look at it. Smell it. Taste it. She never asked me if I wanted it.

She moved me through every step and closed me before I knew it was happening.

No pressure. No pitch. No objection handling.

Just a kid who believed, with her whole body, that I needed to experience the thing she was holding.

That is what we have been talking about for the last 180 pages.

The best close does not feel like a close. It feels like someone who genuinely wants you to experience something good.

When you sit across from a prospect and believe, in your chest, that they need what you have, the conversation goes exactly where it is supposed to go.

The system works. I have watched it work for hundreds of gym owners, trainers, and salespeople across this industry.

It is not theory. I built it in the field. I watched it close deals that had no business closing.

I watched it rescue people who were a month away from shutting the doors.

But the system is only as good as the person running it.

If you went through this book and highlighted everything and filled out every Your Move and then went back to picking up the phone the exact same way you did before, you got nothing out of this.

The change does not happen in the reading. It happens in the reps.

One Assignment For Monday

Not a list. One thing.

Walk into your gym Monday morning and say this to yourself before you touch the phone.

I have everything I need right now. I know my numbers. I know my members.

I know I can help people. Every tool I need is already in my hand.

Then pick up the phone and find the next person you can help.

Not to hit a number. Not to close a deal.

To answer the question you should be asking every single day of your career.

"How do I find the next person who needs what I have, without chasing them, without pressuring them, and without becoming someone I am not in the process?"

That question is the whole book.

Every chapter led here. The calls, the consults, the objections, the close, all of it exists to answer that one question in the moments when it matters most.

You took the biggest risk most people never take. You believed in yourself enough to build something.

Now go run it like you know exactly what you are doing.

Because you do.

Be Needed. Not Needy.

That is the whole lesson from Chapter 1 in four words.

Let them need you. Not the other way around.

I am rooting for you.

— Tom Leonardis Jr.

The Call Script

The full qualifying call, word for word

"Print it. Tape it next to your phone. Use it until you do not need it. Then use it anyway."

Every framework in this book lives here.

This is the full qualifying call, from the first word to the booked appointment.

Print it. Tape it next to your phone. Use it until you do not need it anymore. Then use it anyway.

The Opening

When the prospect picks up, you have about 20 seconds to establish that you are a professional and this call is worth their time. Do not fumble it.

Hey, is this [first name]? This is Leo from [gym name]. You filled out my ad on Facebook the other day and said you wanted some help with your fitness goals. Does that sound familiar?

[Wait for them to say yes. Let them confirm. Do not rush past this.]

Awesome. I just want to understand what is actually going on for you right now so I can see if we can actually help you. You got two minutes?

[Wait for permission. This is not a formality. You are asking them to opt in.]

Belief 1: They Have A Real Problem

You are going to ask two questions. Then you are going to shut up and listen.

Tell me a little bit about what is going on right now. What made you raise your hand on that ad?

[Let them talk. Do not interrupt. Take notes. Listen for emotion, not just facts.]

How long has this been going on for you?

[The answer is always longer than they expect. Let them sit in that for a second before you move.]

Belief 2: They Cannot Fix It Alone

What have you tried on your own before this?

[They will tell you about the diets, the apps, the YouTube videos, the gym membership they never used.]

And how did that go?

[This is a Hell Island question. Let them describe the failure in their own words. Do not help them.]

Belief 3: Doing Nothing Costs More

If you keep going the exact direction you are going for the next six months, what does that look like for you?

[This is the cost of inaction question. This is the one that tips the conversation. Let them answer. Do not fill the silence.]

And how would you feel about that?

[Now they are feeling it. You did not push them there. They walked themselves there.]

Belief 4: A Better Future Is Possible

OK, now flip it. If the next six months went exactly the way you wanted them to go, what does that look like? What is different?

[This is the Heaven Island question. Let them paint the picture. Do not interrupt.]

And how would that feel? What would change in your day to day?

[Watch for energy change in their voice. That is the moment the sale is won, even if they do not know it yet.]

Belief 5: They Can Do This

On a scale of 1 to 10, how important is it to you to get this figured out in the next 30 days?

[Anything below a 7 needs another round of questions. Anything 7 or above means you keep moving.]

Why not a [lower number]?

[This question is magic. They will tell you all the reasons they are ready. You did not sell them. They sold themselves.]

Belief 6: You Are The Right Fit

Here is what we do, real quick, so you know who you are dealing with. We help people like you get [their specific goal] without [the specific fear they just told you about]. We do it by combining training, accountability, and a plan that actually fits your life. Sound like what you are looking for?

[Keep it to three sentences. Do not pitch features. Mirror their own language back to them.]

Belief 7: Now Is The Time

Cool. The next step is a Fitness Vision consultation. It is about 45 minutes, in person, no obligation, no pressure. We sit down, I build you a plan based on what you just told me, and we walk through what it looks like to actually get you there.

I have Monday at 8 AM or Wednesday at 6 PM open. Which one works better for you?

[Two options. Never an open calendar. Let them pick.]

When They Say They Need To Think About It

This is going to happen. A lot. Here is what I say.

I totally understand. Quick question though. Do you need to think about it for two to three days, or two to three weeks?

[They almost always say two to three days. Now they have set their own follow up window. You did not chase them.

They put the stake in the ground.]

OK, so let us do this. I will lock in Wednesday at 6 PM for you, and if anything changes between now and then we can adjust. Fair?

[You booked it. You did not ask permission. You made it easy to say yes and harder to say no.]

When They Say It Is About The Money

I hear you. And honestly, price is important. I would rather you never spend a dollar with us than spend one you regret. Can I ask you this? If money were not the issue, is this something you would want to do?

[This separates money objections from real objections. Most of the time money is the cover story.]

OK, good. Then let us meet Wednesday at 6 PM and I will walk you through what it actually costs and we can see if there is a version of this that works for your budget. Cool?

Closing The Call

Perfect. So Wednesday at 6 PM. I am going to send you a text right now with the address and a confirmation link. Can you reply to it so I know you got it?

[The text confirmation is not optional. It is how you protect your show rate.]

One last thing. I am going to text you again Tuesday night just to make sure we are still good for Wednesday. If anything comes up between now and then just reply to that text and we will figure it out.

Looking forward to meeting you. See you Wednesday.

[End on a forward looking line. Not thank you. Not I appreciate it. See you Wednesday.]

What This Script Does Not Say

Notice what is not in this script.

No price. No packages. No features. No comparison to other gyms. No closing lines about the sale ending Friday.

Everything that would make this feel like a sales call is missing on purpose.

That is the point.

This is not a sales call. It is a qualifying conversation that leads to a booked appointment.

Every word of this script exists to get them through the door. The actual sale happens in the consult.

Run this script until it does not feel like a script anymore. Then run it a hundred more times after that.

The Objection Playbook

Nine objections, three responses each, zero excuses

"Selling is not something you do to someone. It is something you do for someone."

Every objection in this chapter follows the same structure. You get what they say, what they really mean underneath it, three different ways to respond depending on how the conversation is going, and what not to say. The wrong response to an objection does not just fail to close the deal.

It actively makes things worse. Knowing what to avoid is just as important as knowing what to say.

Most objections are not about the thing they claim to be about. Price is almost never about money. Timing is almost never about the calendar.

Spouse objections are almost never about the spouse. Your job is to hear what is underneath the words and respond to that, not to the surface.

"When the pressure is built right, objections are rare. When they do come up, use these."

"It is too expensive."

What they really mean: I am not convinced the result is worth the investment. I am scared to spend money on myself and fail again. I am comparing this to a cheap gym membership or an app that did not work.

Response A — Empathy and Reframe "Totally get that. Appreciate you being upfront with me. So it sounds like you are a little unsure whether the result is going to match the investment.

Is that fair?" Let them answer. Then: "A lot of people feel that way when they first hear the number. They have spent money on things that did not deliver.

So the number feels heavy because of what it represents, not just what it costs. Can I ask you something? What have you already spent over the last couple of years trying to solve this on your own?

Gym memberships you did not use, programs you started and stopped, supplements that did not work?" They will add it up. Usually it is more than your program costs. Then: "So the question is not whether you can afford to invest in this.

The question is whether you can afford to keep getting the same result you have been getting." Response B — Direct Challenge "Let me ask you something straight. If I told you that in six months you were going to drop the weight, get your energy back, and feel like yourself again, what would that be worth to you? Not in dollars. In quality of life." Let them answer.

Then: "Right. So the number we are talking about is actually less than what you just described. The price is not the problem. The certainty is. And that is something we can work through together right now." Response C — Social Proof "I hear you.

Honestly, almost everyone I have ever signed up said the same thing at this point in the conversation. One of my clients, she was in the same spot. Said she could not justify the cost.

Three months in she told me it was the best money she had spent in five years. Not because the number changed. Because her life changed." "The price looks different after the result.

Right now you are paying for a possibility. Six months from now you will be paying for a reality. Most people look back and say the only thing they regret is not starting sooner." What NOT to say: • "I understand, let me see if I can get you a discount." • "Well it is cheaper than a personal trainer." • "We have a payment plan if that helps." The moment you offer a discount before they ask for one, you confirm that the price was negotiable all along.

Hold the price. Defend the value instead. OBJECTION 2

"I need to think about it."

What they really mean: I am overwhelmed. I do not feel enough urgency yet. I am afraid to commit and fail again.

I liked what I heard but I have not been given a clear reason to decide right now.

Response A — Empathy and Clarify "Of course, no pressure at all. Can I ask one thing before you go? What specifically do you need to think through?

Because I want to make sure I gave you everything you need to make a good decision." This works because it separates the objection from the real concern. Most of the time they cannot name a specific thing. That tells you there is no real objection — just hesitation.

When they say "just everything," come back with: "It sounds like it is less about a specific question and more about whether the timing feels right. Is that closer to it?" Now you are talking about the real thing.

Response B — Cost of Delay "I totally respect that. Can I just ask — and be honest with me — when you say you need to think about it, does it feel like a thinking problem or a feeling problem?" "Because here is what I have seen. The people who say they need to think about it almost never come back with a better decision.

They come back with more doubt. The question you are really answering right now is not whether this is the right program. It is whether today is the day you decide to stop waiting.

What would it take for today to be that Response C — Name the Pattern "You know what, I appreciate you being honest. Can I be honest with you? Most people who say they need to think about it have been saying that for months.

Maybe years. About the gym, about their health, about getting started. And every time they think about it, nothing changes. I am not saying that to be harsh.

I am saying it because I hear your goals and I think you are capable of this. What I do not want is for today to be another moment where you walked away from something that could have changed things for you." What NOT to say: • "Okay, no problem, let me know when you are ready." • "Here is my card, call me when you decide." • "I will follow up with you next week." Any version of "let me know" hands over all the control and signals you do not believe the decision is urgent. Keep the conversation going.

Ask one more question. OBJECTION 3

"I do not have time."

What they really mean: I am overwhelmed by my schedule and I have not found a way to prioritize myself. I have tried before and life got in the way. I am afraid to commit to something I might not be able to follow through on.

Response A — Reframe the Time Argument "I hear that. You are busy. Honestly, everyone I work with was busy before they started. But can I ask you something?

How much time are you spending right now feeling tired, frustrated with how you feel, or thinking about this? Because that is time too. And it is not going anywhere." "Most of our members work out three times a week.

Forty five minutes. That is two percent of your week. Two percent for the energy and clarity to handle the other ninety eight percent better. Is two percent actually the problem?" Response B — Build Around Their Schedule "Okay, walk me through your week for a second.

What does a typical Tuesday and Thursday look like for Let them talk. Find the gaps. Then: "So what if we built your entire program around those exact windows? No guessing, no friction, just show up when it already fits.

We work around your life, not the other way around. Would that change things?" Response C — Flip the Priority Can I be direct with you for a second? The people who say they do not have time for their health are usually the same people whose health eventually forces them to make time for it.

Hospital visits, chronic fatigue, injuries that sideline them for months. I would rather you spend three hours a week on your terms than be forced to take a month off on someone else's terms. That is the real time cost of not going.

What NOT to say: • "We offer flexible hours so you can come anytime." • "Even twenty minutes a day can make a difference." • "Lots of our members are busy too." Flexible hours and busy members are features, not responses to an objection. They do not address the real concern which is that they do not believe they can prioritize themselves. OBJECTION 4

"I need to check with my spouse or partner."

What they really mean: I am not sold enough yet to go home and defend this decision. I need more certainty before I can advocate for it. Or: I have already decided but I am using my partner as the exit.

Response A — Respect and Redirect "I totally respect that. Sounds like you and your partner make big decisions together, which I think is great. So it is not a no, you just want to make sure they are on board too." "Here is what I have seen happen.

When someone goes home and says I want to join a gym, the conversation goes one way. When they go home and say I talked to someone today about getting my energy back and feeling like myself again, the conversation goes differently. How would your partner feel knowing this was the reason?" Let them answer.

They will usually tell you everything you need to know.

Response B — Surface the Real Concern "Totally fair. Before you go though, can I ask you one thing? If your partner said yes tonight, is there anything else that would be holding you back?" This is the most important question in this objection.

If they say no, the spouse is the only real issue and you solve it together. If they hesitate or come up with something else, you now know the spouse was a decoy and there is a deeper concern to handle.

Response C — Bring the Partner In "You know what, I love that you want them involved. Why do not we get them on a quick call together? Not a sales call.

Just five minutes so they can hear exactly what we talked about and ask any questions they have. A lot of couples have done it and it just makes the whole thing cleaner. Would they be available sometime this week?" Most of the time they will not take you up on this.

But the offer alone signals you have nothing to hide and changes the dynamic entirely.

What NOT to say: • "Oh no problem, just let me know what they say." • "Here is some information you can show them." • "A lot of people make this decision on their own." Giving them a brochure to take home is giving them permission to disappear. Keep the conversation moving forward. OBJECTION 5

"I want to get in better shape before I start."

What they really mean: I am embarrassed to show up out of shape. I do not want to feel like the weakest person in the room. I am afraid of being judged by people who are further along than I am.

Response A — Name the Irony "I hear that. And I appreciate your honesty. But I want to gently point out something.

You want to get in better shape before you start a program designed to get you in better shape. That is a little bit like saying you want to get healthy before you go to the doctor." "Nobody comes here already in shape. That is exactly what this place is for.

Not what you graduate to once you have figured it out. Everyone in here started where you are right now. Would it help to know that?" Response B — Address the Judgment Fear Directly "Can I tell you what I actually see in this gym every day?

People at every single level showing up, doing the work, minding their own business. Nobody is watching you. Nobody is judging you.

The only people paying attention to you in here are the coaches. And we are paying attention because we want to see you win." "The embarrassment you are feeling right now? It disappears the moment you walk through the door the first time.

Every single client I have ever worked with said the same thing afterward. I was terrified and I cannot believe I almost did not come." Response C — Make It Concrete "Okay, let me ask you this. What specifically would you need to do or look like before you felt ready to start?

Give me the number on the scale or the mile time or whatever it is." Let them name it. Then: "How long do you think it would take you to get there on your own, doing what you have been doing? Because if the answer is more than a few weeks, you are just delaying the thing that could get you there faster.

We can meet you exactly where you are right now. What would it take for that to feel okay?" What NOT to say: • "Oh you look great, you definitely do not need to get in shape first." • "We have all different types of people here." • "Our program is designed for beginners." Telling someone they look great when they have just expressed embarrassment about their body is dismissive. It tells them you did not actually hear them.

Address the fear, not the appearance. OBJECTION 6

"I am afraid I am going to get hurt."

What they really mean: I do not trust my body. I have an injury history that scares me. I do not believe you can keep me safe at my level.

Or: I am using injury fear as a reason to avoid commitment.

Response A — Lead With Safety and Competence "That is one of the most important things you could tell me. Thank you for sharing it. That history does not disqualify you from this.

It just means we need to be smarter about how we build your program." "Can you walk me through what happened? When was it, what specifically was the injury, and where are you with it now?" Let them tell the full story.

Take notes. Then: "Okay. Here is what I want you to know. Every program we build is individualized. We are not putting you through the same thing as the person next to you.

Your history comes with us into every session. That is not optional here." Response B — Reframe Risk "I want to ask you something. What is the risk of not doing anything?

Because injuries do not only happen in gyms. They happen when the body gets weaker, less mobile, less stable. The thing that protects people from injury long term is not avoiding exercise.

It is building the right kind of strength." "The risk of doing nothing is actually higher than the risk of starting with the right people. And you are talking to the right people right now." Response C — Offer a Test Drive "Here is what I want to do. Let us get you in for a movement assessment before we talk about anything else.

Thirty minutes, we look at where your body is, what it can handle, what we need to work around. No commitment. Just information. Then you can make a decision based on what you actually see instead of what you are afraid of. Would that feel like a fair starting point?" What NOT to say: • "Do not worry, we have worked with injured people before." • "Our coaches are certified so you will be safe." • "You can just modify the movements." Vague reassurances do not address a real fear.

Specificity does. Show them you actually understand their history and have a plan for it. OBJECTION 7

"My schedule is too crazy. I travel a lot."

What they really mean: I am afraid I will pay and not use it. I do not want to feel guilty about missing sessions. I have failed at consistency before and I do not want to do it again.

Response A — Build Around the Reality "That makes total sense. You do not want to pay for something and not use it. So let me ask you this.

When you travel, are you always completely unavailable? Or do you have some days where you have mornings free, or evenings?" Let them describe their actual travel schedule. Find the gaps. Then: "So it sounds like the issue is not that you are never available.

It is that you do not want a rigid schedule that collapses the moment your week gets complicated. What if we built something specifically designed to flex with you?

Three sessions when you are home, a remote option when you are traveling. No guilt, no wasted money. Would that work?" Response B — Reframe What Consistency Means "Can I challenge something real quick?

When you say your schedule is too crazy, what I hear is that you are waiting for a perfect week to start being consistent. But that week is never coming. The people who get results are not the people with the easiest schedules.

They are the people who decided that even an imperfect workout counts. Two sessions a week every week beats five sessions a week for three weeks and then nothing."

"What would it look like to commit to just two sessions a week and see how that feels? Because I think you might surprise yourself."

Response C — Remove the All or Nothing Framing "Here is what I want you to hear. The people who travel the most are often our most consistent members. Not because their schedule is easier.

Because they made a decision that this was non negotiable. They work out in hotel gyms. They modify. They do not miss the weeks they are home.

The schedule is not the obstacle. The decision is the obstacle. Have you actually made the decision What NOT to say: • "We are open early and late so you can always find a time." • "You can always make up missed sessions." • "Lots of our members travel." Hours of operation and makeup sessions do not solve a consistency fear.

The fear is about willpower and follow through, not logistics. OBJECTION 8

"I have been burned before. Nothing ever works for me."

What they really mean: I have tried and failed multiple times and I am protecting myself from another disappointment. I believe the problem is me, not the program. I need someone to show me this time is actually different.

Response A — Validate and Differentiate "Thank you for sharing that. I know how frustrating that feels. It sounds like you gave it an honest shot before and did not get what you were promised.

You are not alone in that."

"Can I ask what those other experiences looked like? What did you try, and where did it fall apart?"

Let them talk. Actually listen. Do not interrupt. Then: "So it sounds like the common theme is not that you did not try. It is that you were missing accountability and someone checking on you when things got hard. That is exactly what we do differently.

You will not be handed a program and left alone with it. Every week someone is looking at your results with you." Response B — Put the Problem on the System "Here is the reframe I want to offer you. It was not that nothing worked.

It is that nothing was built for how you actually live. Apps do not call you when you stop showing up. Big box gyms do not notice when you disappear.

You were not the problem. The accountability structure was the problem."

"What would it mean to you if this time someone actually held you to the goal you just told me about? Not as a punishment. As a partnership."

Response C — Make a Direct Commitment "You know what, I appreciate that level of honesty. So let me be honest back. I cannot promise you that this is going to be perfect.

What I can promise you is that we are not going to let you disappear. If you miss a session, we call. If your results are not where they should be, we adjust.

We do not have a business model where you paying and not showing up works out for us. Your results are our

"Given everything you just told me about what has not worked, does that sound different?"

What NOT to say: • "Our program is totally different from anything you have tried." • "I am sure you will love it here." • "You just need to stay motivated." Motivation is the worst thing to bring up here. They have tried motivation. They know it fades.

Accountability and structure are the real differentiators. Lead with those. OBJECTION 9

"Now is just not the right time."

What they really mean: I have not been given enough internal pressure to act right now. I am hoping waiting will make the decision easier. There is something in my life I am using as a reason to delay.

Response A — Name the Pattern Gently "I hear that. Can I ask, when do you think the right time would look like? What would need to be Let them answer.

Usually they cannot name a specific trigger. When they say "just after the holidays" or "when things calm down at work" you say: "Okay, so March. What happens in March that makes this possible that is not possible today?

Because from where I sit, the goals you described are not going to feel any less urgent in March. And the weight is not going to take a vacation until then either." Response B — The Cost of Waiting "I want to ask you something honestly. If you think back to a year ago, were you saying something similar?

That you were going to start when the time was right?" Let them sit with that. Then: "The right time has a funny way of never arriving on its own. It arrives when you decide it does.

What I know is that every month you wait is another month of feeling the way you told me you are feeling right now. Is that a cost you are okay with?" Response C — Create a Specific Anchor "Okay. I want to help you find the right time.

Tell me what is going on in the next four to six weeks that is making this feel bad timing." Let them list it. Then work around it. "So if we start on the fifteenth after that trip, and we build the first two weeks lighter while you find your rhythm, does that feel more manageable?

I can hold that date for you right now if you want to lock it in. That way it is already on the calendar and you do not have to make the decision again." Locking in a future start date is not losing. It is converting a no into a scheduled yes.

Follow up two days before that date.

What NOT to say: • "Okay, no problem, reach out when you are ready." • "We are always here whenever you decide." • "Here is my card." Any response that signals the door is open indefinitely gives them permission to never walk through it. Always leave with a specific next step, even if that step is a future start date.

The Gym Jumper

The gym jumper walks in with a list of every gym they have ever tried. Orange Theory, Lifetime, Planet Fitness, a kettlebell place that closed down, the trainer they used for six weeks three years ago. They say all of this like it is a resume.

What they are really telling you is that they get bored, or things stop working fast enough, and they leave before anything has a real chance to work.

"It sounds like you have tried a lot of things and you keep moving from one to the next hoping something will finally click. But I wonder if the problem is not the programs. I wonder if it is the relationship.

Every time you switch, you lose the context. The coach does not know your history, your limitations, what motivates you, what shuts you down. You start over every time." "What if the missing piece was not a different program but someone who actually knows you?

Because that is what we build here. This is not a facility.

It is a relationship." Then watch how they respond. The gym jumper usually goes quiet at that point because nobody has ever named the real pattern before.

When They Stack Objections

When someone handles one objection and immediately pivots to another the moment you address the first, call it.

"I notice we just handled the money piece and now we are talking about time. When I see someone move from one concern to another like that, it usually means something deeper is going on that they have not said yet. Can I be straight with you?

What is the real reason you are hesitating?" They might get defensive. Let them. Stay calm. Most of the time they will land on the truth, which is that they are scared. Scared to fail. Scared to be judged.

Scared to want something this much and not get it. When they say that out loud, you are no longer handling an objection. You are having a real conversation.

And real conversations close.

One Rule Above All Others

"Never argue with an objection. Agree with it first. Then redirect."

The moment you push back directly on what someone says, you trigger defensiveness and they dig in harder. Lead with agreement. Validate the concern.

Show them you heard it. Then reframe.

I hear you. That makes sense. A lot of people feel that way. And then here is what I have seen.

That sequence — validate, normalize, redirect — works on every objection in this chapter. The specific words change. The structure never does.

The Follow-Up Toolkit

Templates, schedules, and scripts you can use today

"The fortune is in the follow-up."

Everything in this appendix comes from the field. These are the same schedules, scripts, and systems I built for the gyms I worked with over two decades. None of it is theoretical. All of it has been stress-tested on real leads, real calls, and real people who were one follow-up away from changing their lives.

Use what fits. Adapt what does not. But do not skip it.

The 10 Commandments of Follow-Up

1. Always use and follow your follow-up calendar and make sure your automations are up to date.

2. Always test your workflows before sending to your contacts.

3. Never call at the same time twice, especially on consecutive days.

4. Always follow up every phone call with a text.

5. Keep texts short and sweet. Leave the emails for the meat and potatoes.

6. Keep your pipelines organized.

7. Always answer the three main questions.

8. Always say your price points in a range.

9. Always mention the next time you are going to reach out if you do not hear from them.

10. Always book the consultation or the next call on the first phone interaction.

The 28-Day Follow-Up Calendar

Below is a four-week follow-up schedule that maps out exactly when to call, text, email, and leave voicemails. It was built post-COVID, accounting for the fact that your target demographic is now scattered due to work schedules and their kids' activities. Print it. Pin it to the wall. Follow it.

FOLLOW-UP DAILY AGENDA

WEEK	DAY 1	DAY 2	DAY 3	DAY 4	DAY 5	DAY 6	DAY 7
Week 1	1. Call 2. Text 3. Email	4. Email	5. Call 6. Text	7. Email 8. Text	9. Text	10. Call w/ Voicemail	*Nothing*
Week 2	11. Call 12. Text	*Nothing*	13. Email	14. Call w/ VM + Text	*Nothing*	15. Email	*Nothing*
Week 3	*Nothing*	16. Call 17. Text	*Nothing*	*Nothing*	18. Email	19. Text	20. Add to Newsletter
Week 4	21. VM Drop	*Nothing*	*Nothing*	22. Text	*Nothing*	23. Email	24. Text

Notice the pattern: Week 1 is heavy. By Week 3, you are tapering off. By Week 4, it is a voicemail drop and a few texts. The prospect either responds or gets added to your newsletter for long-term nurture. Do not chase. Follow a system.

Weekly Writing Themes

Each week of follow-up has a theme. When you know the theme, you stop staring at a blank screen wondering what to write. Week 1 is about information and social proof. Week 2 introduces scarcity. Week 3 is last chance. Week 4 is the final offer before they move to your newsletter. Here is the breakdown:

WEEK	TOPICS & KEY INSIGHTS
Week 1	*• Information Giving & Gathering* *• Setting the Expectations* *• Social Proof* *If not contacted this week, connection chance drops 50%.*
Week 2	*• Social Proof & Gift Giving with Scarcity* *• Show how you can help (tips, guides)* *If not contacted this week, chance drops another 15%.*
Week 3	*• Full Scarcity and Last Chance* *• Keep or Remove from List Email/Text* *• Added to Newsletter* *If not contacted this week, chance decreases another 30%.*
Week 4	*• Voicemail Drop for New Offer* *• Scarcity (Spot Opened for Previous Offer)* *If no contact this month, expect 3–9 months of silence.*

The statistics in red are not made up. If you do not make contact in Week 1, your chance of connecting within 30 days drops by 50 percent. Every week you wait after that, the number gets worse. Speed matters. Consistency matters more.

Mix Up Your Call Times

Research shows that calling at the same time every day trains people to ignore your number. They see it once, they let it ring. They see it again the next day at the same time, now you are a pest. Vary your timing and you dramatically increase your connection rate.

Recommended time slots:

- Early morning: 7:45 a.m. to 9:00 a.m.
- Midday: 11:00 a.m. to 1:00 p.m.
- Evening: 6:00 p.m. to 9:00 p.m.

If you have more than 30 leads, split them into three groups. Group A gets morning calls first, Group B gets midday, Group C gets evening. Next round, rotate: A moves to midday, B to evening, C to morning. Keep rotating. The leads who never picked up at 9 a.m. might answer at 7 p.m.

The Voicemail-to-Text Play

Most people under 45 do not listen to voicemails. They glance at the transcription, and if it does not grab them, they swipe it away. That means leaving a voicemail by itself is a coin flip at best. The move is to leave the voicemail and immediately follow it with a text.

Here is a template that works:

"Hey [First Name], this is [Your Name] from [Gym Name]. So sorry to bother you—that was me that just called. I had some time before my next appointment. Is there a better time for a quick call to discuss how we can help you?"

Notice what this does. It is short. It acknowledges the missed call. It does not dump your entire offer into a text. And it sets the expectation that you are a real person with a real schedule. That matters.

If they do not respond, try this one the next day:

"Hey [First Name], this is [Your Name] from [Gym Name]. I noticed your interest in learning more about what we do, and I would love to learn more about you. Can we set up a quick call after 5 p.m.? Let me know, and if I do not hear from you, I will reach out around 8 a.m. tomorrow."

You are setting the expectation for the next touchpoint. That single line—"if I do not hear from you, I will reach out around 8 a.m. tomorrow"—tends to prompt a higher response rate. People would rather text you back than get another call.

The Email-Then-Text Campaign

One of the highest-converting sequences I have ever used is dead simple: send an email with all the information, then immediately follow up with a short text that says nothing except "did you get my email?"

The email does the heavy lifting. It contains the offer, the details, and the call to action. Here is an example:

Email:

"Hello [First Name],

We have just 5 spots left for a free 3-week session of small group personal training. If you would like one of these spots held for you, simply respond 'Yes' to this email or the text message you received.

Warm regards,

Coach [Your Name] from [Gym Name]"

Then the text:

"Hey [First Name]! It is [Your Name] from [Gym Name]. I just sent you an email—did you receive it?"

When I used this approach with new leads or past clients, we hit a 50 percent response rate. Of those who responded, 20 to 30 percent converted to booking a reassessment or consultation. Those numbers are not normal in this industry. That is what happens when you make it easy for people to say yes.

Remember: you have already invested time and money acquiring these leads. Your prospective clients are out there looking for help. Fifteen percent of leads make a purchase within 30 days. The remaining 85 percent may become clients over the next ten years—but only if you keep showing up.

Clear Your Head Before You Dial

Follow-up is even more important than having an amazing product because without effective follow-up, who really cares about what you are selling? If you are not following up, who are you truly training?

But here is the part nobody talks about: what happens inside your head before you pick up the phone matters more than the script you use. If you are dealing with personal issues, try writing out your emotions before making calls. Some people call it brain dumping. It helps clear your mind so you can focus on what truly matters—the person on the other end of the line.

Time-block your calls. If you cannot time-block all of them, understand that if you need clients, you may have to work longer and harder. After each call, take a short break to refocus—especially after calls where appointments were not booked. Go back and review what happened. Always record your calls. It is one of the most valuable training exercises you can do, whether the call went well or not.

ABOUT THE AUTHOR

Tom Leonardis Jr. has spent over twenty years inside the fitness industry. He has worked in box gyms, small group personal training studios, large facilities like Equinox, and retail brands including GNC and Vitamin Shoppe. He holds a Master's degree in Exercise Science with a concentration in biomechanics.

The fitness industry can chew you up and spit you out, and it did. Tom has worked under multiple bosses, learned how people think, how they react, how they take feedback, and how they fall apart when nobody is watching. That is what he mastered. Not the theory. The room.

He has never owned his own full blown gym. He could open one tomorrow. But it would take him away from his family, and that is not something he is willing to do. Instead, he built a career helping gym owners run theirs. Every framework in this book was built in the field, stress tested on real calls, and used by real people to save their businesses.

Tom lives in New Egypt, New Jersey with his wife Kristin, their daughter Hailey, and their son Hudson. Everything he builds is so they never have to wonder what it looks like when someone refuses to quit.

To connect with Tom, learn about his sales training programs, or bring him to speak at your event, reach out directly:

tom@tomleonardis.com

(I read every message.)